THE NEW RULES OF MARKETING WARFARE

THE NEW RULES OF MARKETING WARFARE
A Battle Plan for Winning Customers, Scaling Quickly, and Beating Competitors

Kevin McGrew

Published by Game Changer Publishing

Paperback ISBN: 978-1-967424-45-0

Hardcover ISBN: 978-1-967424-43-6

Digital ISBN: 978-1-967424-44-3

GAME CHANGER PUBLISHING

www.GameChangerPublishing.com

Dedication

For every strategist who's stepped onto the marketing battlefield and fought to win.

This is for the thinkers, the doers—the SMAC Marketers.

You know who you are.

Shoot. Move. Adapt. Communicate.

Stay sharp. Stay bold. Stay in the fight.

L.L.T.S. — Long Live The Strategists

SMAC On

READD THIS FIRST

⚔ A Personal Note Before We Begin

Join the Mission. Enter the War Room.

If you're holding this book in your hands right now, it means something.

It means you're tired of throwing marketing dollars into the void.

It means you're done following playbooks written for someone else's battlefield.

It means you're ready to fight smarter—and win.

But here's what I need you to know:

You were never meant to go to war alone.

That's why I created Marketing Warfare HQ—a private community for readers of this book and strategists like you who are choosing to rise above the noise, outthink the competition, and lead their teams and businesses with clarity, courage, and command.

Inside the HQ, you'll meet founders, marketers, and entrepreneurs who speak your language.

Who've walked through the fire.

Who are sharing what works—right now—on the battlefield of business.

When you join, you're not just getting access to a network.

You're stepping into:

- Live tactical briefings and training sessions
- Behind-the-scenes case studies and breakdowns
- Playbooks, templates, and war stories from other SMAC Marketers
- Industry-specific "War Rooms" where we collaborate, solve problems, and adapt in real time
- A chance to connect directly with me and others who are fighting the same fights you are

If this book is the manual, Marketing Warfare HQ is your command center.

I'll meet you inside.

Let's move fast, share intelligence, and sharpen each other. Because the brands that will win tomorrow are the ones preparing for battle today.

📱 Scan the code on this page or go to marketingwarfarehq.com/recruit to enlist.

Let's not just talk about marketing.

Let's SMAC ON.

L.L.T.S. — Long Live The Strategists

— Kevin

Scan the QR Code Here:

Enlist in Marketing Warfare HQ

THE NEW RULES OF MARKETING WARFARE

A Battle Plan for Winning Customers, Scaling Quickly, and Beating Competitors

Kevin McGrew

ACKNOWLEDGMENTS: MY BATTLE BROTHERS & SISTERS

This book would not exist without those who shaped me, inspired me, and stood by me in the darkest hours of my entrepreneurial battles.

To my wife, Tami—My greatest supporter, my rock, my anchor. When I doubted myself, you believed. When I wanted to quit, you stood firm. Every crazy business idea I pursued, you supported. You never wavered—and because of that, I am here today.

To my children, Ashley, Christian, Joshua, and Nathaniel—In my hardest moments, you were my lighthouse. Driving home after brutal days, knowing I'd cross that bridge and see your smiling faces running to greet me, gave me the strength to fight another day. You are my greatest victory.

To my father, Virgil Arlon McGrew Jr.—Your FAW mindset shaped me into the warrior I am today. Your teachings—improvise, adapt, and overcome—are the foundation of this book and the strategy I now pass on to others.

To my mother, Stella Cuevas—A first-generation American who came to this country with nothing but a dream. Your unwavering faith, resilience, and positive energy taught me that no matter how dire the situation, a solution will always present itself if you keep your mindset strong.

To my Bromigos—Darin ("Howie/Mason"), Frank ("Ferdi"), Rangie ("Dawg"), and Greg ("Red")—four of the greatest friends a man could ever have. From childhood to now, we have walked together through every battle—losing family, celebrating milestones, and everything in between. Our annual trips to our little piece of paradise in Mexico on the Rio Hardy are sacred. You are my true battle buddies. LLTB—Long Live The Brotherhood. Because every man needs a Bromigo!

To Jay Conrad Levinson (1933–2013), author of *Guerrilla Marketing*— Your book was my first battle manual. Given to me on my 18th birthday, it lit a fire in me that never went out. *It taught me that marketing is war, and every entrepreneur must be dangerous enough to fight.*

TABLE OF CONTENTS

PREFACE   13

INTRODUCTION   17

PART I: ESTABLISHING THE BATTLEFIELD   23

Chapter 1: The New Battlefield: Why Strategy Beats Size   25

- The Evolution of Digital Marketing Warfare   26
- Why Small Forces Can Defeat Larger Armies   30
- The SMAC Framework: Your Strategic Advantage   33

Chapter 2: Intelligence Wins Wars: The Art of
Knowing Your Market Before You Engage   45

- Understanding Your Combat Zone (Market Analysis)   47
- Identifying High-Value Targets (Ideal Customer Profiling)   50
- Assessing Your Arsenal (Resource Audit & Optimization)   56

PART II: THE SMAC FRAMEWORK IN ACTION   67

Chapter 3: SHOOT—Precision Targeting   69

- Target Acquisition: Finding Your Perfect Customer   71
- Ammunition Conservation: Strategic Budget Allocation   75
- Precision Strike Planning: Campaign Development   79

Chapter 4: MOVE—Tactical Agility   91

- Speed as Your Primary Weapon   94
- Rapid Response Protocols   99
- Strategic Pivot Points   104

Chapter 5: ADAPT—Combat Evolution   115

- Intelligence-Gathering Systems   116
- Battle Damage Assessment (Analytics & Optimization)   120
- Strategic Evolution Framework   124

Chapter 6: COMMUNICATE—Command & Control   135
- Message Clarity and Force Multiplication   137
- Cross-Channel Communication Strategy   142
- Building Your Army of Advocates   147

PART III: ADVANCED OPERATIONS   159

Chapter 7: Special Operations   161
- Combined Arms Marketing (Multi-Channel Integration)   163
- Guerrilla Tactics for Market Penetration   167
- Covert Market Entry Strategies   170

Chapter 8: Securing the Victory   179
- Building Your Marketing Special Forces   181
- The Commander's Strategic Playbook   185
- Future Combat Operations (Emerging Technologies & Trends)   188

Chapter 9: Building Your Digital Arsenal   199
- Your Digital Command Center: Establishing Home Base   200
- Supply Lines and Provisions: Generating Website Traffic   203
- Forward Operating Bases: Social Media Platforms   206
- Secure Communication Channels: Email and SMS infrastructure   208
- Local Territory Control: Dominating Your Geographic Space   210

THE PATH FORWARD: A PERSONAL CALL TO ACTION   231
ABOUT THE AUTHOR   235
ABOUT THE USS LONG BEACH CGN-9   237
THE SMAC MARKETER'S CREED   239
APPENDIX A: Digital Marketing Arsenal Audit Templates   241
GLOSSARY: 100+ Marketing Warfare Terms   253
FINAL ORDERS   275
THE BATTLE CRY: This Isn't Just a Book. It's a Battle Worth Fighting.   277

PREFACE

The Battlefield of Business: The FAW Principle & The SMAC Framework

It is often said that victory is achieved long before the battle ever begins. The same is true in business. You don't step onto the battlefield of entrepreneurship armed only with hope. You need a strategy. You need weapons. You need a battle plan.

This book is that battle plan.

Growing up, both of my parents owned small businesses. I witnessed firsthand the highs and devastating lows. When money was tight, when rent was due, and we didn't know how we'd pay it, my mother never wavered. Her positivity was her weapon—her law of attraction, always bringing a solution even in the hardest times. My father, a Marine, instilled in me a different kind of weapon: the FAW Mindset—Find A Way.

He taught me three immutable rules of battle:

- **Improvise:** Find creative solutions to unexpected problems.

- **Adapt:** Adjust to changing situations.

- **Overcome:** Push through obstacles to accomplish the mission.

These were not just words. They were the way we survived, the way we built, the way we won. That mindset eventually evolved into a full framework—one I now call **SMAC—Shoot, Move, Adapt, Communicate**—the ultimate battle strategy for outmaneuvering and outsmarting bigger competitors.

The Slingshot That Defeated Goliath

Every small business owner knows what it's like to stand before a giant. The Fortune 500 companies, with their limitless budgets. The competitors with bigger teams, better connections, and deeper war chests. It feels impossible. But let me tell you this:

David didn't win with strength. He won with strategy.

David entered the battlefield with just a sling and five smooth stones. Goliath was armored head to toe, weighed down by his strength and confident in his size. But David did not fight Goliath's fight—he fought his own. He used precision (Shoot), agility (Move), adaptability (Adapt), and a clear message (Communicate).

- **SHOOT:** David didn't swing wildly—he aimed. He had one shot, and he made it count. Your business must do the same. Stop throwing marketing dollars in every direction. Target with absolute precision.

- **MOVE:** David did not stand still. He dodged, repositioned, and stayed agile. A small business's strength is its ability to pivot faster than the giants. Use it.

- **ADAPT:** David knew he couldn't win in a battle of brute strength. He changed the game. He turned weaknesses into advantages.

- **COMMUNICATE:** David didn't just kill Goliath—he made a statement. His victory sent a message that shifted the tides of war. Your messaging, your brand, and your presence must strike with that same impact.

Why Small Businesses Win Like David

This Is War—And You Must Be Equipped

Most entrepreneurs don't realize they're stepping onto a battlefield until it's too late. They think they're "starting a business." No, you are engaging in a war for attention, customers, and survival. Most businesses fail not due to a poor product or lack of effort, but because they weren't prepared for the battle ahead.

- 20% of businesses fail in their first year.

- Nearly 50% fail by year five.

- Not because they weren't good. Not because they didn't hustle. But because they walked into war unequipped.

That ends today.

The Final March

I have been writing this book for 20 years. It started as a biography, a letter to my children about the FAW Principle, and survival in business and life. Over time, it evolved into the SMAC Framework—because survival is not enough. You must dominate.

This book is your slingshot. The SMAC Framework is your battle plan. The war for your business is real. Are you ready to win it?

"By the time you finish this book, you won't just be a business owner—you'll be a commander with a winning battle plan."

"Every warrior needs a squad. Join the Marketing Warfare HQ and sharpen your edge with other SMAC Marketers."

QR CODE Here

Enlist Now

Join the HQ | marketingwarfarehq.com

INTRODUCTION

Finding Another Way: From Pizza Flyers to Marketing Warfare

It was July 1978, and I was 12—skateboarding door-to-door in the sweltering Southern California heat, a stack of flyers in one hand and a dream in the other.

Carpio's Pizza—our family's pizzeria in Downey—wasn't going to market itself. While Pizza Hut and Shakey's Pizza were all over TV with flashy commercials and deep-pocketed ad campaigns, I was the one-man marketing department for our little shop. No budget, no TV spots, no billboards—just me, my skateboard, and a mission.

Most people ignored me. Some took the flyer just to be polite. A few slammed doors in my face. But every once in a while, someone made eye contact, took the flyer, and walked into our restaurant later that week. And when my mom told me a customer had come in because of *my* flyer, it lit something inside me.

> *"That was my first taste of marketing. Not in a classroom, not from a book, but in the real world—learning that the right message, in front of the right person, at the right time, could change everything."*

Of course, back then, I didn't call it *marketing*. It was just doing whatever it took to get people in the door. But looking back, that was my first lesson in guerrilla marketing—the art of competing with nothing but creativity, persistence, and sheer willpower.

Semper Fi and Finding Another Way

That lesson was reinforced at home. My dad was a Marine, and if there was one thing he drilled into my head, it was the idea of Semper Fi—Latin for always faithful. But to him, that wasn't just about loyalty to the Corps. It was about staying faithful to the *mission*, no matter what.

Whenever I hit a wall, whenever I thought I was out of options, he'd say, "Don't give up, Kevin. *Find another F*$@! Way.*" That became his mantra. In time, it became mine—with a twist: FAW. Find. Another. Way.

It stuck with me through everything.

When I joined the Navy and had to prove myself—FAW.

When no one was returning my cold calls and I was selling from a storage unit—FAW.

When I started my own company and had to compete against billion-dollar corporations—FAW.

Every time life threw an obstacle in my path, the answer wasn't to back down. It was to adapt. **To think strategically. To pivot. To move faster and smarter than the competition.**

From the CIC to the Boardroom

In 1984, I enlisted in the U.S. Navy, serving under President Reagan when military strategy was evolving fast. I became an Operations Specialist in the Combat Information Center (CIC), stationed aboard the USS Long Beach. Our ship wasn't the biggest or most powerful in the fleet, but we had something just as valuable—intelligence, precision, and adaptability.

We weren't there to overpower the enemy—we were there to *outmaneuver* them.

The CIC was a high-stakes environment where split-second decisions meant the difference between success and disaster. We had to track threats, analyze patterns, and act fast—often before the enemy knew what was happening.

That experience taught me something that changed the way I saw everything: wars aren't won by brute force alone. They're won by strategy.

And what I didn't realize was that the principles of strategic warfare—the very same ones I learned in the Navy—apply just as much to business as they do to combat.

The David Vs. Goliath Business Battle

Fast forward years later, and I found myself in a new kind of battlefield: entrepreneurship.

My company, TechTrack Solutions, had a shot at a massive contract with Yahoo. The challenge? Inventory 500,000 servers across 17 global data centers—in just four months. We were up against IBM and HP Global Services, two behemoths with virtually unlimited resources, entire teams dedicated to winning contracts like this, and reputations that practically guaranteed them the deal.

We were David facing *not one, but two* Goliaths.

But here's the thing: **Goliath always has a weakness.**

The big corporations were like aircraft carriers—powerful but slow. Meanwhile, we were operating like a fast-attack submarine—nimble, precise, able to pivot at a moment's notice.

Instead of trying to beat them at their own game, we redefined the game. We analyzed Yahoo's pain points, found inefficiencies in IBM and HP's approach, and positioned ourselves as the smarter, faster solution.

And we won.

That moment confirmed what I'd been learning all my life: small businesses can win big—but only if they stop playing by the giant's rules. They have to think differently. They have to Shoot, Move, Adapt, and Communicate.

That's when the SMAC Framework was born.

Why I Wrote This Book

I wrote this book because most small businesses don't fail because they have bad products. They fail because they don't understand the battlefield.

They think they're just running a business when, in reality, they're in a war.

- A war against bigger, better-funded competitors

- A war for customer attention in an overcrowded marketplace

- A war against outdated marketing tactics that no longer work

And like any war, victory goes to the side with the best strategy.

If I could travel back and hand my younger self a playbook, this would be it—except I had to live through the war to write it. It's not about throwing more money at ads or blindly copying what big companies do. It's about leveraging your strengths, identifying your enemy's weaknesses, and executing precise, strategic attacks that put you in a winning position.

Inside these pages, you'll discover:

- Why 95% of businesses market the wrong way and how to fix it.

- How to attack market gaps that big companies are too slow to capitalize on.

- Real-world examples of small brands that outmaneuvered giants and the exact steps they took.

- How to create a marketing strategy that actually makes money, instead of just "building awareness."

- The biggest lies the marketing industry tells you—and what to do instead.

The **SMAC Framework** is built on four core principles that determine success in any business:

1. **SHOOT:** Lock onto the right targets. Stop wasting money marketing to people who will never buy.

2. **MOVE:** Be faster and more agile than your competitors. Pivot when they hesitate.

3. **ADAPT:** The battlefield is constantly changing. Learn how to spot threats and opportunities before they hit.

4. **COMMUNICATE:** Control the message. Make sure your brand is heard, understood, and trusted in the market.

This isn't theory. It's not fluff. It's a battle-tested system that has helped businesses punch above their weight class and win.

> *"Small businesses can win—but only if they learn to Shoot, Move, Adapt, and Communicate."*

This book is divided into three parts: establishing your battlefield, deploying the SMAC Framework, and running advanced operations. Each section contains real-world stories, strategy breakdowns, and a key takeaways section for each chapter. I have created a learning enhancement package and it is available for download in the Marketing Warfare HQ (our online community) to turn theory into action.

If you've ever felt outgunned, outspent, or outmatched, this book will show you how to turn the tide.

Because you don't need the biggest budget to win, you just need the smartest strategy.

The battlefield has changed. The old rules don't work anymore. Are you ready to fight smarter? Then let's go to war!

FAW Forward!

Kevin McGrew

Founder, CEO & Chief Strategist, Everzocial

Creator, The SMAC Framework

PART I: ESTABLISHING THE BATTLEFIELD

CHAPTER 1

The New Battlefield:
Why Strategy Beats Size

"Victorious warriors win first and then go to war, while defeated warriors go to war first and then seek to win."
—Sun Tzu, *The Art of War*

Mission Brief: CHAPTER 1 – The New Battlefield: Why Strategy Beats Size

This isn't business as usual—it's war. And on today's battlefield, the size of your company matters far less than the sharpness of your strategy. You don't need more money—you need better moves.

Your mission:

Shift your mindset from marketing to maneuvering. Smaller, more agile businesses are already beating the giants—and you can, too. This chapter introduces the SMAC Framework and prepares you to think like a strategist, not a spender.

Welcome to the digital battlefield—where small businesses fight giants every day. This isn't just a struggle for attention—it's a fight for survival.

Businesses are launching campaigns every day, fighting for visibility, and deploying strategies to win over customers. Some will succeed. Many will fail.

"The difference? Those who understand the new rules of marketing warfare."

My transition from the Navy to entrepreneurship and into the world of marketing was a profound revelation. The same principles that dictated success in military operations—strategy, adaptability, precision, and resilience—became the foundation for how I survived and grew in business.

In the Navy, we understood that victory wasn't reliant on having the largest arsenal or the most firepower. It was about strategic precision—leveraging intelligence, moving decisively, and striking with purpose.

The Navy taught me something the business world often forgets: victory doesn't go to the biggest—it goes to the smartest. In both war and business, success is a matter of strategy, not size.

The same holds true in the digital age. Smaller businesses can absolutely win, but only if they stop trying to fight a war they aren't equipped for. Most entrepreneurs make the fatal mistake of copying larger competitors—trying to match their marketing budgets and playbooks. You can't win by fighting on their terms. You must redefine the battlefield, rewrite the rules, and execute with surgical precision.

Imagine stepping onto a battlefield where your enemy has tanks, air cover, and unlimited resources. If you charge headfirst, armed with only a rifle and sheer determination, you're walking into a massacre. By understanding their weaknesses and acting quickly, you can defeat even the strongest opponent by attacking when they're least ready.

This book is your battle plan—to help you outmaneuver, outthink, and outfight competitors with deeper pockets and louder voices. You will learn to master the SMAC Framework—a powerful strategy honed from extensive experience in both the military and the competitive world of digital marketing—to decisively shift the odds in your favor.

This is your war. Your battlefield is set. By the end of this book, you'll have the strategies, tactics, and mindset to claim victory.

The Evolution of Digital Marketing Warfare

The rules of marketing have changed. The battlefield has shifted; it's no longer determined by the largest budget or the loudest voice. Now, success hinges on expertly navigating the digital landscape with precision, agility, and strategic insight. The days when large corporations could dominate simply by throwing money at billboards, TV ads, and radio spots are gone.

Today, the marketing war is waged online, where agility and intelligence matter more than brute force.

To understand this shift, consider David vs. Goliath, but with a modern twist. In the past, Goliath—the Fortune 500 companies—controlled the battlefield with mass media dominance.

But the rise of digital marketing has armed David, the small and mid-market businesses, with tools that can deliver highly targeted strikes, often at a fraction of the cost. The battlefield has become asymmetric, favoring those who can outthink rather than outspend their opponents.

From Mass Marketing to Micro-Targeting

In the early days of advertising, success was about reach. Brands measured their marketing effectiveness by the number of people they reached through TV, print, or radio ads. The more people saw the message, the better, regardless of how relevant those people were.

But digital marketing changed the game. The rise of search engines, social media, and data analytics shifted the focus from mass exposure to precise audience targeting. Today, businesses can analyze consumer behavior, track interactions, and serve hyper-personalized ads to the exact people most likely to convert.

A small, local coffee shop struggled to compete against large, national coffee chains. Instead of focusing on mass advertising, they focused on local digital engagement. Through the strategic implementation of targeted social media content, geo-targeted advertisements, and an engaging email loyalty program, they successfully boosted foot traffic by an impressive 30% in just six months. Their success stemmed from enhanced engagement with their audience, not increased spending.

Speed Over Size: Why Agility Wins

A key evolution in digital marketing warfare is the importance of agility. Large companies struggle with slow decision-making and bureaucratic layers, while smaller businesses can pivot quickly. This is especially crucial in a world where algorithms, trends, and consumer preferences shift overnight.

A family-owned party rental business successfully competed against a larger, more established rival by implementing an e-commerce strategy.

This included online ordering, a cleanliness guarantee, and expanded offerings for commercial customers. These changes led to a 50% sales increase within a year, highlighting the potential for quick growth by adapting to new business models and customer needs.

For businesses today, the lesson is clear: adaptability is a competitive advantage. If your marketing strategy is rigid and slow, you'll get left behind.

Data: The New Weapon of Choice

In past marketing eras, businesses relied on gut instinct, vague demographics, and rough estimations to shape their campaigns. Now, data rules everything. Companies that harness data effectively can make smarter, faster, and more profitable marketing decisions.

Fashion Nova, a clothing boutique founded in 2006 in Los Angeles, has effectively competed with major online retailers through e-commerce and influencer marketing. Transitioning to an online platform in 2013, the boutique engaged customers via social media, collaborating with influencers on Instagram and TikTok to drive remarkable growth.

By focusing on authentic content creation instead of traditional marketing, Fashion Nova connected well with its audience, significantly increasing online visibility and sales. They tracked product engagement with strategic hashtags like #novaswim and #fashionnovacurve using real-time customer insights and a smart content organization system. This allowed them to refine their marketing approach based on direct customer feedback, resulting in over 21 million Instagram followers and 4 million TikTok followers.

The boutique's journey from a single store to a billion-dollar business illustrates how effective social media use and genuine influencer partnerships can challenge larger brands, proving that small retailers can thrive by fostering authentic customer relationships.

Even small businesses can use data to compete effectively. Tools like Google Analytics, Meta Ads, and CRM software help companies analyze customer behavior, manage advertising budgets, and enhance messaging in real time.

The Power Shift: Customers Now Control the Narrative

Another major shift in digital marketing warfare is who holds the power. In the past, brands controlled their reputation through advertising and PR. Today, customers control the conversation.

- 90% of consumers read online reviews before making a purchase (BrightLocal).

- User-generated content (UGC) performs 4x better than brand-created content (*Adweek*).

- Influencer marketing delivers 11x higher ROI than traditional forms of marketing (TapInfluence).

This means that marketing is no longer just about broadcasting messages— it's about building relationships, earning trust, and creating shareable experiences. Companies that adapt to this shift not only survive but thrive. Those who ignore it become obsolete.

The Digital Battlefield Demands a New Strategy

Winning in today's marketing landscape requires a different kind of thinking. It demands a shift from traditional, one-size-fits-all marketing to precision-driven, data-backed, and highly adaptable tactics. It's no longer about how much money you can spend, but how effectively you can deploy your resources.

The War Is Won by Those Who Adapt First

Digital marketing is changing fast. If you're still stuck using old tactics, you will get left behind. But if you adapt with the right strategies and move quickly, you'll come out on top.

Whether you're an entrepreneur, marketer, or business executive, your survival hinges on mastering this shift. The digital battlefield is relentless, but with the right strategy, you will turn the tide in your favor.

It's time to stop playing by old rules. The battlefield has changed. Have you?

Why Small Forces Can Defeat Larger Armies

Throughout history, it has been demonstrated that smaller, more agile forces can triumph over even the strongest armies. Their victories are achieved not through brute strength but through strategic thinking, adaptability, and exceptional tactics.

The same holds true in business today. The old rules, where big companies dominated with large ad budgets and wide distribution, no longer apply. The battlefield has shifted, and with the right approach, small and mid-market businesses can compete and actually win.

Leveling the Playing Field

In the Battle of Agincourt in 1415, the outnumbered English army, led by King Henry V, faced off against the heavily armored French forces. The French knights, confident in their superiority, expected an easy victory.

But Henry V had something they didn't—tactical innovation. The English used longbows and strategic positioning to overcome the French's numerical advantage, resulting in a crushing defeat.

This same principle applies in today's modern marketing environment: strategy trumps size. Businesses using modern tools like AI-driven insights, targeted ads, and real-time analytics can surpass larger competitors.

A Real-World Example of Outsmarting the Giants

Looking back on my early days in business, my company, TechTrack Solutions, competed against KPMG and Telus Enterprise Solutions for an asset-tracking contract with Electronic Arts (EA).

On the surface, it appeared to be a classic David versus Goliath scenario—our competitors wielded immense resources and extensive experience. Rather than trying to compete on their level, we focused on EA's unique challenges, developing a solution specifically tailored to their needs.

The result? We successfully secured the contract—not due to our size, but because of our intelligence, agility, and deep understanding of the client's true requirements.

AI and Digital Tactics: The Longbow of Modern Marketing

If AI and digital tools are the game-changers in the new rules of marketing warfare, ignoring them is like showing up to a fight with a stick while your competition has a gun. The companies that win today are those that:

- Use AI-powered analytics to understand their audience better than ever before

- Leverage automation to engage customers at the right time with the right message

- Deploy hyper-targeted advertising instead of wasting resources on mass marketing

A family-owned beauty brand harnessed the power of AI-driven social listening tools to pinpoint emerging skincare trends, which empowered them to introduce niche products ahead of their bigger rivals. This savvy strategy allowed them to capture market share that larger competitors had overlooked.

Speed and Adaptability Win Modern Wars

The Battle of Trenton in 1776 is one of history's greatest military upsets, showcasing George Washington's brilliance as a commander. By decisively defeating the well-trained German Hessians, who fought for the British, Washington demonstrated that strategic ingenuity could overcome brute strength.

Understanding that a direct confrontation would be catastrophic, he executed a bold plan with precision, launching an unexpected assault right after Christmas when the enemy was truly unprepared. His swift maneuvers and keen ability to exploit vulnerabilities not only marked a turning point in the conflict but also reinvigorated the morale of his troops and set the stage for future successes.

Small businesses can use a similar strategy. Unlike large corporations with slow decision-making and rigid structures, small and mid-sized businesses can quickly adapt their strategies and seize new trends faster than their competitors.

A home improvement company I worked with adapted quickly when a cold snap hit. While larger competitors stuck to their planned ads, this small business promoted draft-stopping window solutions that homeowners needed right away. As a result, they gained a lot of market attention while competitors fell behind.

Customer Relationships: The Small Business Secret Weapon

An undeniable advantage of smaller forces in warfare—and business—is their capacity to forge stronger relationships with their people. The Mongols, despite being vastly outnumbered by their enemies, demonstrated this brilliantly under Genghis Khan's leadership. They built highly loyal and cohesive military units, enabling them to strike efficiently and precisely.

In marketing, small businesses have the unique advantage of forging deeper, more authentic connections with their customers. Unlike large corporations that often appear distant and impersonal, smaller brands excel at engaging in meaningful conversations, personalizing their messaging, and cultivating loyalty that competitors simply cannot purchase with ad spend.

A specialty coffee brand increased its repeat customers by 40% in a year by creating a loyal community through social media and customer engagement. This strategy focused on niche loyalty rather than mass appeal, helping them compete with national chains.

How You Can Win in the New Age of Marketing Warfare

1. **Think Like a Strategist**—Don't try to fight a battle you can't win. Find the weaknesses in your competitors' approach and exploit opportunities they overlook.

2. **Use Modern Tools**—AI, automation, and data analytics give you the advantage of intelligence and precision. Use them.

3. **Move Faster than the Competition**—Trends shift quickly. Small businesses that adapt faster than corporate giants will always have an edge.

4. **Win on Relationships, Not Just Reach**—The loyalty of a devoted customer base is more powerful than a million disengaged followers.

5. **Leverage Niche Markets**—Big brands cast a wide net, but small businesses can dominate highly specific customer needs with tailored offerings.

Victory Belongs to Those Who Fight Smarter

The new rules of marketing warfare are not about who spends the most—they are about who executes the smartest. If you're willing to embrace modern tactics, use AI and automation, move quickly, and build strong relationships with your audience, you can do more than just compete with the giants.

You can beat them.

Welcome to the new battlefield. The question is: Are you ready to fight?

The SMAC Framework: Your Strategic Advantage

In marketing, like in a battle, being strategic is often more important than being big. The SMAC Framework—Shoot, Move, Adapt, Communicate—is a secret weapon for businesses that want to beat their bigger competitors. It was created based on real-life experiences, and it helps companies create smarter and more effective marketing strategies.

Why You Need a Framework for Marketing Warfare

Great military leaders always step onto the battlefield with a robust plan. They recognize that victory in war transcends brute force; it requires precise execution, agility, and strategic positioning. This principle is equally valid in business. Many businesses falter in their marketing efforts simply because they lack a solid framework that directs their decisions and actions effectively.

The SMAC Framework isn't just another marketing theory. It's a battle-tested approach to modern marketing that helps businesses maximize their resources and execute with precision. Each pillar—Shoot, Move, Adapt, and Communicate—uniquely ensures victory.

Shoot: Precision Targeting Wins Battles

In combat, wasting ammunition can be deadly. The best marksmen don't shoot recklessly; they carefully take one accurate shot.

In marketing, many businesses fail because they use a spray-and-pray approach—launching broad campaigns that try to appeal to everyone. This wastes resources and produces poor results. Businesses should identify their ideal target audience and tailor their messaging to them.

Example: The Power of Precision

WWAKE, a boutique jewelry brand based in Brooklyn, was at a crossroads while competing against mainstream jewelry giants. Recognizing the increasing awareness among millennials regarding environmental sustainability and the impact of fashion, WWAKE boldly chose to realign its brand strategy.

They stopped broad marketing and embraced their identity as a female-owned, sustainable jewelry maker by partnering with like-minded influencers who valued environmental care and ethical practices.

The brand emphasizes authenticity by using eco-friendly packaging and openly communicating its production processes from its Brooklyn studio, which focuses on reducing waste in each piece.

Their focus on recycled gold and local economic growth strongly appealed to environmentally conscious millennials. This authentic approach to sustainability and targeting like-minded consumers significantly increased market share in the competitive jewelry industry, showing that a values-driven strategy can effectively compete with larger retailers.

Move: Agility Beats Size

In warfare, a nimble and agile fighting force can wield a significant advantage over a larger, more unwieldy army. A large army can be intimidating, but it is often vulnerable to a smaller, well-trained unit that can quickly adapt and strike unexpectedly.

Moreover, in the corporate landscape, major companies often become mired in bureaucratic processes that impede their agility in responding to market demands. Small and mid-sized businesses can quickly adapt their strategies thanks to their access to real-time data and inherent flexibility.

Example: Quick Execution Wins the Day

Pete's Real Food saw rising demand for keto meals and moved fast. While bigger players hesitated, Pete's overhauled their menu, introduced flexible ordering, and carved out a niche in the keto market. Their speed—and commitment to customer needs—became their competitive edge.

Adapt: Flexibility Ensures Survival

In war, no plan survives first contact with the enemy. Successful individuals and organizations stand out because they can adapt to changing circumstances and adjust their strategies accordingly.

This principle is equally applicable in marketing, where consumer behaviors are in a perpetual state of change. As trends evolve rapidly and algorithms undergo frequent updates, businesses must stay vigilant and responsive. Companies that cling to outdated strategies will struggle, while those that embrace adaptability and innovation will succeed in a changing market.

Example: A Bakery's Digital Transformation

When the pandemic forced businesses to adapt, Magnolia Bakery made a bold pivot to e-commerce, transforming its operations and expanding its reach far beyond its iconic New York storefront.

Recognizing the growing demand for online accessibility, the bakery launched a seamless digital platform that allowed customers nationwide to order their famous banana pudding and other treats. This shift proved to be a game-changer, generating $10 million in revenue within 11 months and driving a 39% increase in email marketing conversion rates. By focusing on personalized customer experiences and leveraging data-driven insights, Magnolia Bakery successfully built a thriving online presence.

The e-commerce success didn't just boost sales—it elevated the brand's recognition to new heights. Magnolia expanded its offerings into grocery stores, airports, and platforms like Amazon Fresh, making their products more accessible than ever.

With over 2,000 grocery store placements and 432% year-over-year growth in shipments, the bakery became a household name across the U.S. This strategic pivot not only helped them weather the challenges of the pandemic but also solidified their reputation as an innovative and adaptable brand that could meet customers wherever they were.

Communicate: Owning the Narrative

Wars aren't just won on the battlefield—they are won in the minds of people. Whoever controls the narrative controls the war.

Marketing is no different. The businesses that tell the best story, create emotional connections, and establish authority in their industry will dominate.

Many businesses mistakenly believe that just having a good product is enough. It's not. If your audience doesn't know, trust, or believe in your brand, they won't buy. Your ability to engage, educate, and connect with your market determines your success.

Example: Building a Movement, Not Just a Brand

In a world of high-gloss fitness chains and cut-throat pricing wars, mActivity in New Haven dared to be different. Rather than competing on membership fees, this innovative gym reimagined what a fitness community could be, creating an environment where acceptance and connection matter more than mirror selfies and protein shakes.

Their revolutionary approach transformed the traditional gym layout into a social hub, deliberately designed to spark conversations and forge friendships between members who might never have connected otherwise.

The results of this bold strategy speak volumes: while other gyms struggle to keep members beyond their initial contract, mActivity boasts an astounding 98% retention rate. Even more remarkably, when faced with the need to raise prices by nearly 50%, their members didn't flee—they stayed, understanding that their membership represented more than just access to exercise equipment. It was their ticket to belonging to a genuine community. With 62% female membership and 13% of members actively participating in social events, mActivity proved that building a movement around inclusivity and authentic connection isn't just good for the soul, it's good for business too.

Why the SMAC Framework Works

The power of the SMAC Framework lies in its ability to align marketing efforts with business goals while adapting to modern challenges.

1. **It eliminates wasted marketing spend** by ensuring every dollar is strategically invested.

2. **It gives businesses a clear competitive edge** by allowing them to move faster than corporate giants.

3. **It focuses on what truly matters**—engaging the right customers, adjusting to trends, and communicating effectively.

Deploying the SMAC Framework in Your Business

Winning in modern marketing warfare requires a **disciplined, strategic approach**. As you apply the SMAC Framework, ask yourself:

- Are we targeting the right audience or just casting a wide net?

- Can we move faster than our competitors when trends shift?

- Are we adapting to market changes or stuck in outdated tactics?

- Is our brand message strong enough to create a lasting impression?

The businesses that embrace Shoot, Move, Adapt, and Communicate will dominate the digital battlefield. Those that don't? They will be left behind.

Marketing Is Warfare—It's Time to Fight Smart

The SMAC Framework is not just a marketing strategy; it's a mindset shift. It's about thinking like a strategist, executing like a tactician, and always staying ahead of the competition.

Victory in marketing doesn't go to those who spend the most but to those who fight the smartest.

Welcome to the battlefield. Are you ready to deploy SMAC and win the war for your business?

You've seen the battlefield. Now it's time to gather your intelligence.

Real-World Case Study: Stone Brewing— Outmaneuvering Giants in the Craft Beer Battlefield

In the early 1990s, the beer industry was controlled by large brewing companies with big budgets and extensive distribution, making it hard for smaller competitors to succeed. Enter Stone Brewing, a scrappy craft beer company from San Diego, California, with a bold vision: to disrupt the market with high-quality, unapologetically unique craft beers.

Stone Brewing didn't have the financial muscle to outspend industry heavyweights like Budweiser and Miller. Instead, they embraced agility, precision, and adaptability—principles that align perfectly with the SMAC Framework.

Shoot: Precision Targeting

Rather than trying to appeal to mass-market beer drinkers, Stone Brewing zeroed in on a niche audience: craft beer enthusiasts who craved bold flavors and were willing to pay a premium for quality.

Their flagship beer, Arrogant Bastard Ale, wasn't just a drink—it was a statement. With slogans like "You're Not Worthy," they created a rebellious, exclusive identity that resonated with their target audience and distinguished them from mainstream brands.

Move: Tactical Agility

Stone Brewing capitalized on its small size to quickly adapt to emerging trends. They experimented with new beer styles, seasonal releases, and collaborations with other craft breweries.

When the IPA craze began to take off, Stone didn't just join the trend; they led it, introducing some of the most celebrated IPAs in the market. Their ability to pivot and innovate kept their loyal fans engaged while attracting new ones.

Adapt: Combat Evolution

As the craft beer industry exploded, Stone Brewing continually refined its approach. They used real-time feedback from tastings, online reviews, and social media to tweak recipes, packaging, and marketing strategies.

By listening to their customers and adapting to their preferences, Stone maintained relevance and became a trendsetter in the industry.

Communicate: Command & Control

Stone Brewing mastered the art of storytelling and brand advocacy. They used their website, social media, and in-person events to share their mission of challenging the status quo and supporting independent breweries.

Their transparency about their brewing process and commitment to sustainability built trust and loyalty among their customers. More importantly, their bold, unapologetic voice made them memorable.

Outcome

Today, Stone Brewing is one of the most successful craft breweries in the world, with distribution in all 50 states and over 40 countries. They achieved this without ever competing directly on the same playing field as the beer giants.

Instead, they used precision targeting, agility, adaptability, and clear communication to carve out their own space in the market—a quintessential example of how smaller players can win by playing smarter, not bigger.

> *"Lesson? They didn't spend their way to success—*
> *they outmaneuvered their competition with speed,*
> *authenticity, and smart targeting."*

This case study encapsulates the essence of Chapter 1 of the SMAC Framework: the battlefield isn't always fair, but with the right strategy, smaller forces can defeat larger armies. Stone Brewing's story shows how focusing on your unique strengths and staying agile can turn a seemingly insurmountable challenge into a recipe for success.

Just scratched the surface?

Scan here to get your Intel Brief: war-tested frameworks,

bonus guides, and early access drops.

Get Your Intel Brief

Chapter 1 Key Takeaways
The New Battlefield: Why Strategy Beats Size

"You don't need a bigger army. You need a better plan."
—Kevin McGrew

KEY LEARNING POINTS

❖ **Marketing is Warfare—And the Rules Have Changed**

This isn't the old-school marketing playbook. The biggest budget doesn't guarantee victory anymore.

Winning today isn't about brute force—it's about strategy, speed, and precision. If you're not thinking like a battlefield commander, you're already losing.

❖ **The SMAC Framework: Your Tactical Advantage**

The **SMAC Framework—Shoot, Move, Adapt, Communicate**—is built for businesses that want to outmaneuver bigger, slower competitors.

- **Shoot**—Target your ideal customers with precision.

- **Move**—Stay agile, pivot fast, and outflank the competition.

- **Adapt**—The battlefield changes daily; your strategy must too.

- **Communicate**—If your message isn't clear and compelling, no one listens.

❖ **Small Businesses Can Win—If They Play Smarter**

> *"David can still beat Goliath. But only if he outthinks, outmoves, and outmaneuvers him."*

- Your advantage isn't size—it's speed, strategy, and execution.

- You don't need the biggest budget—you need the best tactics.

- If you can't outspend competitors, outstrategize them.

◆ Data is Your New Ammunition

In modern marketing warfare, decisions based on guesswork will kill your business.

- Track everything—customer behaviors, conversion data, competitive moves.

- Analyze fast—use real-time data to adjust campaigns in the moment.

- Stop relying on gut instinct—the best marketers are intelligence-driven.

Your Customers Are the New Generals

The power dynamic has shifted—customers now control the battlefield.

- Social proof, reviews, and word-of-mouth determine your brand's success.

- The brands that listen, engage, and build trust will win.

- If you're not actively managing your reputation, you're at the mercy of the market.

◆ The War is Won by Those Who Fight Smarter, Not Harder

> *"The businesses that dominate aren't the ones that shout the loudest or spend the most. They're the ones that plan better, execute smarter, and adapt faster."*

Action Steps to Prepare for Marketing Warfare

- **Audit your current marketing strategy.** Are you executing with precision or wasting resources?

- **Define your ideal customer.** If you're marketing to everyone, you're marketing to no one.

- **Analyze your competitors.** What gaps can you exploit? Where are they vulnerable?

- **Commit to agility.** If your business can't pivot fast, it's already at a disadvantage.

- **Master the SMAC Framework.** Every decision should be guided by Shoot, Move, Adapt, Communicate.

Final thought: *"In battle and in business, intelligence wins long before the first shot is fired. The war is won in the recon. Victory doesn't belong to the biggest company, but to the smartest, fastest, and most strategic competitor. Are you ready to fight smarter? The war is won by those who adapt first. Marketing today is a battlefield."*

The **SMAC Framework** is your **tactical edge**—use it to execute with precision, dominate your niche, and outmaneuver slow-moving industry giants.

The rules have changed. Your competitors won't wait. It's time to fight smarter, move faster, and win the war for attention, loyalty, and growth.

CHAPTER 2

Intelligence Wins Wars: The Art of Knowing Your Market Before You Engage

"If you know the enemy and know yourself,
you need not fear the result of a hundred battles."
—Sun Tzu, *The Art of War*

Mission Brief: CHAPTER 2 – Intelligence Wins Wars: The Art Of Knowing Your Market Before You Engage

You can't win a war you don't understand. Charging ahead without intel is how empires fall, and campaigns fail. Strategy begins with sight.

Your mission:

Gather the intelligence. Know your enemy, terrain, and resources before making a move. This chapter gives you the tools to understand your market, profile your ideal customer, and assess your position—so when it's time to strike, you're aiming with precision, not guessing in the dark.

The Power of Intelligence in the War of Business

"Business is war. Marketing is a battlefield."

Imagine leading troops into enemy territory—with no map, no satellite feed, and no clue what's ahead. That's what it's like running a marketing campaign without intelligence.

The Breaking of the Enigma Code: The Ultimate Business Intelligence Lesson

During World War II, British intelligence cracked the infamous Enigma code, shifting the course of the war. The German military believed they had an unbreakable cipher—a machine-generated encryption system that changed daily, making their communications impossible to decode. Every troop movement, submarine deployment, and strategic maneuver was disguised in what was thought to be an impenetrable veil of secrecy.

But the British knew that brute force wouldn't win this battle. They needed intelligence, not firepower.

Enter Alan Turing and his team at Bletchley Park, a small yet brilliant group of mathematicians, cryptographers, and linguists. Instead of attempting to manually decipher messages, they built a machine capable of detecting patterns, breaking the code, and deciphering German war plans in real time.

The result? The Allies gained critical intelligence that helped them intercept enemy movements, preempt attacks, and ultimately win the war. Historians estimate that breaking the Enigma code shortened the war by at least two years, saving millions of lives.

Now, what does this have to do with business and marketing? Everything.

Business is war. Marketing is a battlefield.

Just as the British cracked Enigma to outmaneuver the enemy, you must decode your market before your competitors do. If you rely only on traditional methods—brute-force marketing, mass advertising, or following outdated strategies—you're fighting blind. Instead, you must build your own intelligence network, track market signals, decipher competitor strategies, and identify patterns that reveal unseen opportunities.

> *"Like Turing's team at Bletchley Park, your business doesn't need unlimited resources—it requires the ability to outthink, outmaneuver, and out-strategize the competition."*

This chapter arms you with the tools to analyze competitors, identify market gaps, and refine your customer profiling strategies. By the end of this section, you won't just be reacting to the market—you'll be dictating its terms.

i. Market Recon: Understanding Your Combat Zone (Market Analysis)

Why Knowing the Battlefield Gives You the Upper Hand

Imagine you're a scout in unfamiliar territory. You don't need to know the whole path—just where to step next. In business, this intelligence comes from market analysis—an in-depth look at who you're up against and where your opportunities lie.

A *Harvard Business Review* study found that 85% of successful businesses attributed their wins to superior market intelligence. They didn't wait for trends to emerge; they anticipated them.

Here's how you can do the same:

1. Identify Key Competitors

- **Who are they?** Research your direct and indirect competitors. Who holds the largest market share? Who is gaining traction?

- **What are their strengths and weaknesses?** Look at their marketing, product offerings, and customer service. What are they doing well, and where are they vulnerable?

- **How do they position themselves?** What key messages do they use? Are they focused on price, quality, speed, or innovation?

Example: A small tech start-up analyzed the crowded mobile app space. They discovered competitors obsessed over flashy features but ignored usability. By creating a simple, frictionless interface, they captured 40% market share in six months.

2. Analyze Market Trends:

- **Where is the market heading?** Follow industry reports, Google Trends, and AI-powered tools like Crayon and SimilarWeb to track real-time changes.

- **What customer pain points are emerging?** Look at online forums, reviews, and feedback loops to understand new customer frustrations.

- **What innovations are disrupting the industry?** Which technologies are reshaping customer expectations?

Example: A local gym realized that traditional memberships weren't enough. By tracking trends, they pivoted to hybrid in-person and virtual coaching, growing their membership base by 200% in a year.

3. Pinpoint Consumer Needs and Desires:

- **Go beyond demographics.** Instead of just identifying age, location, and income, dig into psychographics.

- **Find what emotionally drives your customers.** What keeps them up at night? What are they trying to achieve?

- **Use behavioral data.** How do customers interact with your brand? What purchase patterns are emerging?

Example: A boutique fitness studio found their members struggled with motivation. Instead of generic ads, they created community-driven challenges and accountability groups, leading to a 75% retention rate.

4. Map Out Potential Opportunities and Threats

It's essential not only to grasp the current market dynamics but also to foresee future opportunities and challenges. Engaging in scenario planning and conducting thorough risk assessments empowers you to prepare for a range of potential outcomes. Identifying potential market or competitive landscape changes allows you to develop contingency strategies that keep your business agile and resilient amid uncertainty.

Example: In the early 2000s, as the construction industry continued its traditional path of resource-intensive practices, Kirei's founder, John Stein, observed a growing disconnect between modern design aspirations and environmental consciousness.

While larger corporations viewed sustainable building materials as a niche market, Stein saw an opportunity in combining eco-friendly materials with modern design. He found that the industry's resistance to change posed a threat, making it vulnerable to changing consumer values and stricter environmental regulations.

Within this threat, a remarkable opportunity emerged: the chance to innovate a new category of building materials that would appeal to both design professionals and eco-conscious consumers.

This insight led Kirei to develop innovative products from unexpected sources: bamboo, reclaimed coconut shells, and recycled PET materials.

The company's strategic foresight proved prescient as the sustainable building movement gained momentum throughout the 2010s and into the 2020s.

While competitors struggled to adjust their products, Kirei formed solid relationships with architects and designers who prioritized sustainability and aesthetics. Kirei turned market threats into opportunities, becoming a trusted source for eco-friendly materials and creating a protective advantage through innovative product development and knowledge of sustainable design. Their success shows that analyzing market threats can uncover hidden opportunities for companies willing to challenge the norm.

As you immerse yourself in market analysis, remember it's an ongoing process. Markets are dynamic, and staying informed requires continuous effort. Regularly revisit your analysis, update your insights, and refine your strategies to stay ahead.

Understanding your combat zone lays the groundwork for effective decision-making and strategic execution. This knowledge empowers you to navigate challenges with confidence and seize opportunities with precision. It equips you with the foresight to anticipate shifts in the landscape and the flexibility to respond proactively.

As we move forward in this exploration, keep in mind that the market is not your adversary—it's your arena. With the right insights and strategic acumen, you can turn this arena into a platform for growth and success. The intelligence you gather here lays the groundwork for the next steps in the SMAC Framework, leading you toward marketing mastery.

Use this knowledge as your guide to navigate the challenges of the digital world. Remember: Agility always beats size.

Intelligence Gathering in Action

Your Mission: Over the next 72 hours:

1. **Conduct a deep-dive competitor analysis** using one new tool (Google Trends, SEMrush, Ahrefs, SpyFu, or SimilarWeb).

2. **Interview five ideal customers** to uncover hidden pain points.

3. **Map out one market gap** your business can exploit immediately.

Final thought: *"Marketing isn't about guessing. It's about gathering intelligence, adapting, and executing with precision. The businesses that win in today's digital battlefield aren't the biggest—they're the smartest."*

Are you ready to dominate your market with superior intelligence? The next section will take you deeper into high-value targeting, where the real battles are won.

ii. Target Profiling: Identifying High-Value Targets (Ideal Customer Profiling)

The Cost of Poor Targeting

In both war and business, misdirected efforts waste resources and harm morale. Poor targeting in marketing results in wasted money and missed opportunities. A CB Insights study showed that 42% of failed start-ups blamed their downfall on "no market need." They didn't fail due to a bad product, but because they didn't understand their ideal customer.

A business that effectively identifies and engages its target audience will consistently outperform competitors who rely on guesswork. The secret to success lies in customer intelligence—deeply comprehending your audience at a strategic level.

Why High-Value Targets Matter

Not all customers are created equal. Some are more profitable, loyal, and likely to become brand advocates. Your goal is to identify and prioritize these high-value targets—the customers who deliver the best return on investment (ROI) and long-term growth.

Think of your market like a battlefield:

- **Your ideal customers are your primary objective.** They drive the most revenue and engagement.

- **Your secondary targets may be occasional buyers.** They require more effort to convert but can still be valuable.

- **Your non-targets are distractions.** They drain resources and rarely convert.

Focusing your efforts on **high-value targets** means **less wasted effort, higher ROI, and stronger brand loyalty.**

Building a Laser-Focused Customer Profile

To create a solid, ideal customer profile, you mix data with a bit of gut feeling. Here's how you can build a profile that really brings your marketing game to life:

1. Gather Demographic & Psychographic Data

Demographics are the who—basic identifiers like age, gender, income, and location. But psychographics reveal the why—your customers' motivations, values, pain points, and behaviors.

Demographics:

- Age
- Gender
- Income level
- Location
- Occupation

Psychographics:

- Lifestyle habits
- Core values (e.g., sustainability, affordability, quality)
- Pain points (e.g., time constraints, lack of expertise, need for convenience)
- Buying behaviors (e.g., impulse shopper vs. researcher)
- Content preferences (e.g., blogs, social media, email newsletters)

Example: In 2021, Wild Clean didn't just launch another "green" product—they built a movement. Their insight? Eco-conscious consumers weren't just shopping sustainably—they were desperate to fight the plastic crisis. Founded by self-described "recovering polluters," they tapped into the mindset of the eco-furious—people craving tangible impact. By positioning as the world's first plastic-negative cleaning brand, Wild Clean offered more than products—they offered action.

Within 18 months, their dissolvable powders and forever bottles built a loyal following of parents and millennials who saw their purchase as a protest. Wild Clean didn't just sell cleaners—they sold a cause.

2. Define Your Customer's Pain Points and Aspirations

Customers don't buy products. They buy solutions to problems or ways to achieve their goals.

Ask yourself:

- What problems keep your ideal customer up at night?
- What obstacles do they face when trying to solve those problems?
- What goals do they aspire to, and how can your business help them get there?

Example: In 2014, Outdoor Voices saw a disconnect in fitness culture: while major brands pushed "no pain, no gain," everyday people felt intimidated and left out. Their research revealed a desire for acceptance, comfort, and motivation—not elite performance.

So, they flipped the script. With the motto "Doing Things Is Better Than Not Doing Things," Outdoor Voices championed movement for everyone. They launched inclusive campaigns, designed comfy athleisure for real life, and built a community that celebrated everything from dog walks to casual yoga.

The result? A fast-growing brand that proved meeting people where they are beats pushing them to be something they're not.

3. Build detailed customer personas

Customer personas are detailed, research-backed representations of your ideal customers, focusing on psychographics, motivations, and goals. Understanding them allows for tailored marketing strategies and personalized approaches, moving away from generic methods.

Built on solid research, these personas reflect real customers, enhancing engagement and satisfaction. Personalization can boost customer engagement by up to 500% and satisfaction by 90%, fostering relationships that lead to loyalty. We'll discuss customer or buyer personas in detail in Chapter 3, but it's important to understand the concept now.

Persona Template:

- **Name:** Sustainable Sarah
- **Age:** 32
- **Occupation:** Environmental Consultant
- **Pain Points:** Struggles to find genuinely eco-friendly products; skeptical of "greenwashing"
- **Buying Motivations:** Prioritizes ethical sourcing, sustainability, and minimal waste
- **Preferred Channels:** Instagram, ethical shopping blogs, word-of-mouth recommendations
- **Key Message That Resonates:** "Skincare that's as kind to the planet as it is to your skin."

Example: In 2011, HelloFresh entered a crowded meal-kit market filled with generic "home cooking made easy" messaging. But through customer research, they found a goldmine: young professionals who wanted to cook healthy meals but were stuck in 50+ hour workweeks and a cycle of takeout.

They focused on this persona—"the Aspirational Health-Conscious Professional"—and built their strategy around it: 30-minute recipes, dietitian-approved meals, mobile-first ordering, and influencer partnerships that matched their audience's lifestyle.

With targeted messaging like "From phone to fork in 30 minutes," HelloFresh didn't try to reach everyone—they just deeply understood the right someone. That focus helped grow their customer base from 280,000 to over 7.5 million.

4. Where to Find Your Ideal Customers

Once you know **who** your high-value customers are, you must **find where they spend their time**.

- **Social Media Preferences:** Are they active on Instagram, LinkedIn, TikTok, or YouTube?

- **Search Behavior:** Do they research products via Google, Reddit, or niche forums?

- **Buying Channels:** Do they prefer in-store shopping, e-commerce, or subscription models?

- **Engagement Preferences:** Do they respond best to email marketing, webinars, or influencer recommendations?

Example: In 2019, CycleBoard struggled to differentiate itself in the competitive electric mobility market while managing a tight marketing budget. Instead of resorting to conventional paid advertising methods, they harnessed a valuable insight about their early adopters: their customers were not merely riders but passionate advocates eager to showcase their CycleBoards to friends and family. This observation led to a pivotal strategy shift.

The company launched a straightforward but powerful referral program that turned their existing customers into a passionate sales force. They turned casual chats about their unique three-wheeled electric scooters into a real income by offering a 10% PayPal cash reward for successful referrals.

The strategy was remarkably effective, resulting in over $700,000 in referral sales within just 18 months. This impressive figure represented nearly 10% of all transactions, achieved at a fraction of the cost of traditional advertising methods. The strategy shows that gaining new customers can be more effective through genuine recommendations from satisfied customers rather than wide-ranging marketing campaigns.

5. Validate & Evolve Your Customer Profiles

Customer preferences change. Your profiles should **never be static**—they must evolve based on real-time data.

- **Track engagement metrics**: What content gets the highest clicks, shares, and conversions?

- **Monitor buying patterns**: Are seasonal trends emerging? Are certain demographics shifting?

- **Collect direct feedback**: Use surveys, reviews, and social listening tools to stay connected.

- **Refine your personas regularly**: Adjust messaging, channels, and strategies as new insights emerge.

Example: A SaaS company regularly surveys customers to identify pain points. They found that users wanted better onboarding tutorials, so they revamped their email sequence with personalized product walkthroughs, reducing churn by 30%.

Final Mission: Sharpen Your Targeting Strategy

Your Mission: Over the next 72 hours:

1. Create a detailed persona for your high-value customer. Include demographics, psychographics, pain points, and buying habits.

2. Use a tool like Google Analytics or Facebook Audience Insights to refine your target audience.

3. Identify three new ways to reach your ideal customer. Whether it's influencer partnerships, niche forums, or social media engagement, find where they are and meet them there.

Final thought: *"Your marketing should never be broad or generic. The more you refine your high-value targets, the more effective your campaigns will be. Businesses that thrive don't just find customers—they understand them better than anyone else."*

Are you ready to dominate your market with precision targeting? The next section will dive into assessing your arsenal, knowing exactly what resources you have to execute your strategy flawlessly.

iii. Assessing Your Arsenal (Resource Audit & Optimization)

Why Your Resources Are Your Greatest Weapon

A skilled general never sends troops into battle without assessing their arsenal. They take stock of weapons, supplies, manpower, and strategic positioning.

In business, your arsenal consists of your financial resources, marketing tools, human capital, and operational capabilities. Knowing what you have—and optimizing how you use it—determines whether you will execute effectively or run out of firepower when it matters most.

Many businesses fail not because they lack potential, but because they misallocate resources.

- They overspend on low-impact marketing channels.

- They invest in expensive technology that they don't use to its full potential.

- They underutilize their best employees, leaving key strengths untapped.

A strategic resource audit ensures that every dollar, tool, and team member is working toward victory.

Conducting a Full Resource Audit

Before optimizing, you must assess what's in your arsenal. Break it down into four key categories:

1. Financial Resources: Where Is Your Money Going?

⊘ **Marketing Budget Allocation:** Are you investing in high-ROI channels or spending blindly?

⊘ **Advertising Efficiency:** Are your ads bringing in qualified leads or generating clicks with no conversions?

⊘ **Operational Costs:** Where can you streamline expenses without sacrificing quality?

⊘ **Revenue Streams:** Are you maximizing profit opportunities, or are you overly dependent on one income source?

Example: When Seltzer Goods saw their wholesale business collapse, they didn't panic—they focused. Instead of spreading budget thin, they went all-in on one thing: cold-audience Facebook ads using a "See, Think, Do" framework.

The results? A 785% revenue jump, 9.68x ROAS, and a cost-per-customer of just $4.87. But it didn't stop there—brand searches surged 931%, Instagram referrals soared 1,700%, and conversion rates across channels skyrocketed up to 903%.

The lesson? Sometimes doing one thing extremely well beats doing everything okay.

2. Marketing & Technology Stack: The Tools of War

Your marketing technology should serve your strategy, not complicate it. Assess:

⊘ **Website Performance:** Is your website fast, mobile-optimized, and conversion-friendly?

⊘ **CRM & Email Marketing Tools:** Are you leveraging automation, segmentation, and personalization?

⊘ **SEO & Content Marketing:** Do you have a clear content strategy, or are you creating content without direction?

⊘ **Paid Media & Social Advertising:** Are your ad platforms generating measurable ROI?

⊘ **Analytics & Data Tracking:** Are you tracking the right metrics or relying on vanity numbers?

Example: In the bustling corridors of Thermo Fisher Scientific, a familiar scene played out: marketers juggling multiple platforms, struggling to extract value from a tangled web of marketing tools. Each business unit operated in its own digital silo, with teams only scratching the surface of their technology's potential. The wake-up call came when leadership realized they were paying premium prices for overlapping capabilities while utilizing just a fraction of each tool's features.

The transformation began with a bold vision: create a Marketing Center of Excellence to streamline their tech stack. By methodically consolidating their marketing systems and establishing a central marketing group, Thermo Fisher didn't just cut costs—they revolutionized their entire approach.

The results spoke volumes: marketing teams finally had the bandwidth to master their tools, leading to a dramatic improvement in campaign effectiveness, faster sales cycles, and a remarkable reduction in cost per lead. What started as a cost-saving initiative evolved into a masterclass in marketing efficiency, proving that sometimes less really is more in the world of marketing technology.

3. Human Capital: Maximizing Your Team's Strengths

Your **team is your most valuable resource.** Misalignment of roles and underutilization of strengths **can cost you growth.**

- **Skill Set Evaluation:** Are team members working in roles that align with their strengths?
- **Delegation & Outsourcing:** Are you focusing your team on high-impact tasks while outsourcing low-value activities?
- **Leadership & Decision-Making:** Is your leadership structure efficient, or are bottlenecks slowing execution?
- **Training & Development:** Is your team evolving with industry trends and new technologies?

Example: LeadChat's live chat tool was generating 4–8x more leads than traditional methods—but their sales experts were buried in daily operations, not scaling the business.

The fix? They brought in a virtual assistant—not as a patch, but as a strategic growth lever. The VA documented processes, built training systems, and freed up the core team to innovate.

The result? LeadChat expanded into 10 countries, serving hundreds of new clients. By reallocating human capital, they didn't just save their growth—they unleashed it.

4. Operational & Competitive Positioning: Are You Battle-Ready?

- **Customer Experience Optimization:** Are your customer service processes streamlined and efficient?

- **Competitive Advantage Assessment:** How do your resources compare to your competitors?

- **Scalability & Adaptability:** Can your current operations handle rapid growth or sudden changes in demand?

- **Risk Management:** Are you prepared for industry disruptions, supply chain issues, or market downturns?

Example: Thrive Market entered the e-commerce grocery space with explosive growth—up to 50% month-over-month—but early success exposed a major vulnerability: their manual, small-scale fulfillment couldn't meet surging demand.

Instead of patching problems, they went all-in on scale. Thrive opened massive fulfillment centers in Indiana and Nevada, adopted automated warehouse systems, and used AI forecasting tools like RELEX to streamline inventory and delivery.

The transformation worked. Today, they ship over 4,000 orders daily with a 90% two-day delivery rate, proving that operational intelligence isn't just backend—it's a battlefield advantage.

Optimizing Your Resources for Maximum Efficiency

Once you've audited your resources, it's time to **optimize for efficiency, impact, and scalability.**

1. Reallocate your budget for maximum ROI

- Identify underperforming expenses and cut them.

- Double down on high-ROI marketing efforts.

- Invest in automation tools that reduce manual work.

- Test new acquisition channels in controlled experiments.

Example: A SaaS company cut ineffective display ads and shifted its budget to high-intent LinkedIn campaigns, increasing enterprise client sign-ups by 35%.

2. Maximize the value of your existing tools

- Eliminate redundant software and consolidate tools.
- Ensure team members are fully trained on tech platforms.
- Automate repetitive tasks to free up human capital.
- Use AI-driven analytics for smarter decision-making.

Example: A real estate firm automated lead follow-ups with AI-driven chatbots and increased client response rates by 60%.

3. Strengthen your team and improve leadership efficiency

- Delegate low-impact tasks and focus on core competencies.
- Upskill your team with regular training.
- Hire or outsource specialists to fill skill gaps.
- Create a culture of agility and rapid decision-making.

Example: A consulting firm outsourced content writing to focus on high-value client strategy, leading to a 30% increase in billable hours.

4. Future-proof your business against market shifts

- Monitor competitor moves and market trends regularly.
- Stay adaptable with contingency plans in place.
- Build relationships with multiple suppliers to prevent disruptions.
- Develop a data-driven approach to forecasting and decision-making.

Example: A DTC brand used AI-powered demand forecasting to predict seasonal sales trends, reducing inventory waste by 25% and increasing profitability.

Final Mission: Strengthen Your Arsenal

Your Mission: Over the next 72 hours:

1. **Audit your marketing spend** and cut at least one underperforming expense.

2. **Optimize your tech stack**—eliminate or consolidate redundant tools.

3. **Delegate or automate** one repetitive task to free up your team's focus.

4. **Identify and improve one inefficiency** in your operational process.

Final thought: *"The businesses that win in competitive markets aren't the ones with the most money—they're the ones that use their resources the smartest."*

Are you ready to optimize your arsenal and execute with precision? The next chapter will take you into tactical deployment, where intelligence meets action and strategies turn into victories.

Real-World Case Study: Spotify— Understanding the Battlefield to Dominate Music Streaming

In 2006, the music industry was in chaos. Illegal downloads via Napster and torrenting were rampant, while giants like Apple's iTunes tried to monetize music through individual song purchases.

Daniel Ek, a Swedish entrepreneur, saw a gaping opportunity: people didn't want to own music—they wanted access to it. Armed with this insight, Ek founded Spotify, a music streaming platform that would redefine how the world consumes music.

But the path to success was anything but smooth. Spotify faced titans like Apple, entrenched record labels, and consumer skepticism. So, how did they win? By mastering every element of battlefield intelligence.

Understanding the Combat Zone (Market Analysis)

Spotify began with a sharp analysis of the market's pain points. Consumers were frustrated with paying for individual songs or albums on platforms like iTunes and equally dissatisfied with the low-quality, risky nature of illegal downloads.

Meanwhile, artists and record labels were losing billions to piracy. Spotify identified a middle ground: a platform offering legal, unlimited, high-quality music streaming, supported by advertising and subscription revenue.

Spotify also understood the timing. Faster internet speeds and the rise of smartphones made streaming feasible. Instead of competing with iTunes on downloads, they focused on access, introducing a subscription model that gave users unlimited music on demand—a revolutionary concept at the time.

Identifying High-Value Targets (Ideal Customer Profiling)

Spotify didn't try to *target everyone*. Their initial focus was on young, tech-savvy users already consuming music through torrents or platforms like LimeWire. These users valued convenience and quality but were reluctant to pay for music. Spotify's freemium model—offering free ad-supported streaming alongside a premium subscription option—was tailor-made for this audience.

By converting free users into paid subscribers through features like offline listening and ad-free streaming, Spotify created a sustainable growth funnel. This precise targeting allowed them to build a loyal user base while refining their product for broader appeal.

Assessing Your Arsenal (Resource Audit & Optimization)

Spotify knew they couldn't compete on hardware like Apple or established music catalogs like record labels. Instead, they focused on building a superior user experience powered by cutting-edge technology. Their primary assets were their engineers, who developed an innovative peer-to-peer streaming technology that reduced server costs while delivering high-quality audio.

They partnered with labels, offering fair royalty payments—something piracy never could. By aligning with the music industry rather than fighting it, Spotify gained access to extensive catalogs and legitimacy.

Executing the Strategy

Armed with this intelligence, Spotify launched in 2008, first targeting the European market where piracy was rampant. Their freemium model allowed users to experience the platform risk-free, while premium subscriptions drove revenue. Spotify used data to refine its offering, introducing personalized playlists like Discover Weekly, which became a game-changer in music discovery.

By 2011, Spotify expanded to the U.S., where it faced Goliaths like Apple and Pandora. But their data-driven approach and user-centric features helped them carve out a loyal audience. By offering a better experience than free torrents and more convenience than purchasing music, Spotify turned skeptics into fans.

Victory on the Battlefield

Today, Spotify is the world's leading music streaming service, with over 500 million active users and 200 million paid subscribers. Their success lies in their mastery of battlefield intelligence. By understanding the market, identifying high-value targets, and optimizing their resources, Spotify not only survived the music industry's upheaval, they thrived.

Spotify's journey demonstrates the power of Chapter 2's principles. Success doesn't come from trying to fight every battle—it comes from understanding where to strike, how to strike, and whom to fight for. Through precision and insight, Spotify turned a fragmented market into a global empire. Their story serves as a powerful reminder: **intelligence is the ultimate weapon** in any David vs. Goliath battle.

Chapter 2 Key Takeaways: Intelligence Wins Wars: The Art of Knowing Your Market Before You Engage

"In business, like in combat, the smartest fighters win long before the first shot is fired. They win in the recon."
—Kevin McGrew

KEY LEARNING POINTS

◆ **The Power of Intelligence in Business Warfare**

Marketing is a battlefield, and intelligence is your secret weapon. Just like in war, the businesses that win aren't always the strongest or the best-funded—they're the ones with superior battlefield intelligence. If you don't understand your market, your competitors, and your customers, you're fighting blind.

◆ **Lessons from the Breaking of the Enigma Code**

During World War II, British intelligence cracked Germany's Enigma code, giving the Allies a decisive advantage. They didn't win by brute force—they won by outthinking the enemy. Your business needs the same mindset: outmaneuver your competitors with intelligence and strategy, not just effort.

◆ **Understanding Your Combat Zone (Market Analysis)**

Before launching a campaign, you need deep market intelligence. This means:

✅ Knowing your direct and indirect competitors.

✅ Identifying your industry's key trends and shifts.

✅ Understanding consumer pain points, desires, and decision-making processes.

✅ Recognizing market gaps that big players are too slow to act on.

◆ Identifying High-Value Targets (Ideal Customer Profiling)

Most businesses fail not from lack of effort—but from poor targeting. You can't hit what you can't see. You must:

- Pinpoint your most profitable, engaged customers.
- Understand their challenges, buying habits, and motivations.
- Attract your best-fit customers—instead of chasing anyone with a wallet.
- Speak their language and align your messaging to their values.

◆ Assessing Your Arsenal (Resource Audit & Optimization)

"Victory isn't about having unlimited resources— it's about using what you have with military precision."

Audit your:

- **Financial resources:** Are you spending on the right marketing channels?
- **Technology stack:** Are your tools effective or slowing you down?
- **Human capital:** Are the right people doing the right jobs?
- **Competitive positioning:** How do your resources compare to your competitors'?
- **Scalability:** Can your business handle rapid growth and change?

◆ The War is Won by Those Who Adapt First

The businesses that dominate markets are **not the biggest—they're the fastest learners.** Use real-time data, customer insights, and competitor intelligence to pivot before your competitors do.

◆ Action Steps to Strengthen Your Battlefield Intelligence

- ✅ Conduct competitor analysis using tools like Google Trends, SEMrush, and SimilarWeb.

- ✅ Identify three new market gaps or opportunities your competitors are missing.

- ✅ Refine your ideal customer profile using real purchase behavior and engagement data.

- ✅ Audit your current marketing spend and cut at least one ineffective expense.

- ✅ Implement a tracking system for customer feedback and competitive intelligence.

Final thought: *"Your business isn't failing because of a lack of effort—it's failing because you don't have the right intelligence to guide your attacks."*

*"Stop wasting resources on blind marketing.
Know your enemy, know yourself, and fight smarter."*

PART II: THE SMAC FRAMEWORK IN ACTION

CHAPTER 3

Shoot—Precision Targeting

"The aim of marketing is to know and understand the customer so well the product or service fits them and sells itself."
—Peter Drucker

Mission Brief: CHAPTER 3 – SHOOT: Precision Targeting

Spray-and-pray marketing is for rookies. In modern warfare—and in business—every shot must count. Wasting ammo isn't just inefficient; it's fatal.

Your mission:

Identify your ideal target with ruthless clarity. Craft messages that land. Deploy campaigns with accuracy and purpose. This chapter shows you how to aim before you fire—because in the digital battlefield, precision isn't optional—it's your greatest advantage.

Now we shift from intelligence gathering to calculated action—the moment where strategy becomes firepower. It's time to hone your targeting, where every move is deliberate, every decision strategic.

"Just as a marksman takes their time to line up the perfect shot, your marketing efforts must be precise and intentional."

This chapter is about ensuring that every effort hits its mark, maximizing impact, and minimizing waste.

On one critical naval mission, we had to locate and track a high-value target in a crowded sea, with minimal resources. Firepower wasn't the answer. Precision was.

In today's marketing combat zone, precise targeting is crucial. We need to connect deeply with our audience, moving beyond generalizations to reach those who reflect our brand values.

Each campaign should be sharply focused on our ideal customers, capturing their attention and inspiring action. Now is the time to refine our approach and make every message impactful!

This chapter will guide you through the art of precision targeting, starting with target acquisition. Identifying your perfect customer is the first step, requiring a keen understanding of who they are and what they need. It's not just about who they are or what they think—it's about grasping their aspirations and challenges, positioning your brand as the solution they seek.

We'll discuss how to allocate marketing resources wisely, ensuring every dollar is an investment in meaningful engagement. By understanding which channels and messages provide the highest return, you can outsmart competitors focusing solely on volume.

This chapter will focus on strike planning, which involves creating data-driven and innovative campaigns. A winning campaign is like a precision strike: carefully timed, laser-focused, and devastatingly effective. It demands foresight, adaptability, and a strong commitment to quality.

Take, for example, a small start-up that succeeded by precisely targeting eco-conscious, tech-savvy consumers. Facing tough competition from larger brands, they focused on this niche market and created impactful campaigns. This approach built a loyal customer base and increased their market share without needing large budgets.

This journey into precision targeting isn't just about acquiring customers—it's about building lasting relationships. Each interaction becomes an opportunity to understand your audience better, refine your messaging, and enhance your offerings. It's about creating moments of connection that lead to sustained engagement and advocacy.

As we delve into this crucial chapter, it's imperative to recognize that precision is nonnegotiable. This isn't just a suggestion—it's the key to transforming marketing from a broad exercise into a highly focused operation.

It's imperative to refine your targeting immediately to significantly increase your chances of success and elevate the quality of your engagement. It's essential for your brand to forge a deep connection with those who matter most, and time is of the essence. Take action now!

This chapter is about getting you up to speed using the SMAC Framework. We'll make sure you can turn your marketing goals into actual results. By being purposeful and strategic, your marketing will go from basic campaigns to awesome growth and real connections.

You've gathered the intel. You know the terrain. Now it's time to lock on and pull the trigger.

Mission I: Target Acquisition (Audience Clarity)

At the heart of precision targeting lies target acquisition—the essential process of pinpointing your ideal customer with remarkable clarity. This is not merely a task; it is a strategic initiative that forms the bedrock of your marketing efforts. Much like a master navigator plots a route using exact coordinates, your path to connecting with your audience commences with a deep understanding of who they are and what captivates their interests.

Starting a journey without knowing your destination greatly reduces your chances of success. In marketing, your destination is your ideal customer— those who value your offerings and can contribute to your business with their loyalty and support.

During my time in the Navy, I remember a crucial mission focused on identifying our target. We needed to retrieve important intel from a covert sea operation and had to rely on limited and fragmented reports to find our objective. Our success depended on gathering and interpreting the right information. Our precise approach helped us find our target, showing that knowing your goal is key to success.

In the fiercely competitive landscape of marketing, this means identifying and engaging your target audience effectively. This process is systematic and complex, going beyond basic demographics to reveal valuable insights about your ideal customer. We'll discuss how to identify high-value targets to make your marketing efforts effective and efficient.

Define Your Value Proposition

To identify your ideal customer, you first need to understand what makes your product or service unique. Your value proposition is the foundation upon which customer acquisition is built. It articulates the benefits and features that differentiate you from competitors and resonate with your target audience. Defining this value proposition helps you assess potential customers, ensuring their needs align with your offerings.

This SaaS company has effectively defined its ideal customer profile and created a tailored solution for that market. Pneumatic systems quietly revolutionized workflow automation, changing how small businesses manage their daily operations.

Founded in 2019 by former small-business owners familiar with the challenges of costly automation tools, Pneumatic adopted a unique approach. The company was founded because existing solutions were too complex for nontechnical users or too expensive for small businesses. Their response was to create an intuitive platform that made automation accessible to everyone, regardless of technical expertise.

Pneumatic stands out for its user-friendly interface, allowing small business owners to create complex workflows easily, like arranging sticky notes on a board. At $99 per month, they are making advanced features accessible to small businesses, which were once only affordable for large enterprises.

The platform has notable success stories, such as a Cincinnati bakery that automated its ordering system, cutting errors by 75%, and a marketing agency that regained 20 hours a week by reducing manual tasks. Pneumatic offers a blend of accessibility, affordability, and functionality, showing that effective automation tools can be simple and cost-effective.

They didn't just build a product—they built it for someone. By knowing their customer's pain (complex, overpriced automation), they delivered simplicity with a price tag small businesses could handle. That's the power of precise value alignment.

Develop Detailed Customer Profiles

Building on the groundwork laid in the previous chapter, creating detailed customer profiles is essential for precision targeting. This involves segmenting your audience based on shared characteristics and behaviors, then developing personas that embody these segments. Each persona should capture your ideal customer's motivations, challenges, and aspirations to help create personalized marketing messages.

Stone Brewery exemplifies this perfectly. By creating personas like "Adventurous Alice," a 28-year-old who loves the outdoors and values local ingredients, they tailored their campaigns to showcase regional hops and collaborations with local farmers. This approach not only attracted Alice but also resonated with a broader audience sharing her values.

Leverage Data and Analytics

In today's digital age, data is a treasure trove of insights waiting to be mined. Utilize analytics to track customer behavior, preferences, and engagement patterns. This data-driven approach helps you better understand your audience, ensuring your marketing targets those most likely to convert. By analyzing this information, you can identify trends and adjust your strategies to align with evolving customer needs.

A fashion e-commerce brand found that most of its website traffic came from mobile devices. Armed with this insight, they enhanced their mobile shopping experience, resulting in increased engagement and sales conversions.

Conduct Market Research

Market research is a powerful tool for uncovering hidden opportunities and insights into consumer behavior. Through surveys, focus groups, and social listening, you can deepen your understanding of your target audience and their preferences. This research helps validate your assumptions, ensuring your marketing strategies are grounded in real-world data and insights.

Consider a small organic skincare brand that conducted focus groups to explore consumer preferences. The insights showed a high demand for sustainable packaging, leading the brand to include it in its product line. This attracted eco-conscious consumers and differentiated the brand from competitors.

Test and Refine Your Approach

Target acquisition is not a static process but an ongoing endeavor. Test different messages, channels, and approaches to see what resonates most with your audience. Use A/B testing to compare variations, analyze the results, and refine your strategies accordingly. This iterative process ensures your marketing efforts remain relevant and effective, continually aligning with the evolving needs of your audience.

A digital marketing agency utilized this approach by testing different content formats with their target audience. They found that video content had better engagement and feedback than other formats, prompting a shift toward more effective marketing campaigns.

Cultivate Authentic Engagement

Beyond identifying your target audience, the ultimate goal is cultivating authentic engagement. This means building relationships based on trust, transparency, and mutual value. Engage with your audience through personalized interactions, addressing their needs and providing solutions that resonate with their aspirations. By fostering meaningful connections, you transform prospects into loyal advocates.

A boutique fitness studio forges strong connections with its members by crafting individualized fitness journeys. They fostered a strong sense of community and loyalty beyond the gym by recognizing individual goals and offering personalized support.

The journey to acquiring your perfect customer is as much about precision as connection. Understanding your audience and their values is essential for fostering engagement that promotes business growth. This process helps you gain insights to create effective marketing campaigns.

As we continue exploring the SMAC Framework, remember that successful target acquisition is a blend of art and science. It's about balancing data-driven insights with human intuition, ensuring every interaction is rooted in understanding and empathy.

Understanding your ideal customer and engaging strategically can transform your marketing from mere transactions to building lasting relationships that drive your brand's success.

Prepare to harness these insights as you advance through the SMAC Framework, transforming knowledge into action and strategy into success. The path to precision targeting is yours to navigate, leading your brand confidently toward its goals.

Mission II: Ammunition Conservation (Budget Allocation)

Once you thoroughly understand your target audience, the next step in precision targeting is to optimize your resources by strategically allocating your budget. In marketing, as in any operation with limited resources, efficiency is key. It's not about how much you spend, but how wisely you allocate your budget to achieve maximum impact. This section dives into the art of making every dollar work harder, ensuring that your investments yield the greatest return.

Looking back on my early days in business, I recall the relentless pressure to maximize our limited resources. One particular project with a growing nutraceutical start-up stands out.

The company had a limited budget but big goals. The challenge was to make marketing spending effective to attract attention and acquire customers for their innovative products. My agency used strategic thinking and careful planning to focus resources on high-impact areas and reduce less productive projects. This approach transformed what seemed like constraints into catalysts for growth.

In marketing, budget allocation is like playing chess; every move needs careful thought, and each decision is important. We'll explore how to turn your marketing spending into a strategic investment for your brand's future instead of seeing it as just an expense.

Set Clear Objectives

Before allocating your budget, define clear and measurable goals and objectives. Having a clear goal helps decide how to allocate resources, whether it's for brand awareness, sales, or entering new markets. This clarity ensures that every dollar spent matches your goals, driving efforts toward achieving specific outcomes.

Take, for example, an online sporting goods retailer that aimed to increase new customer acquisitions by 20% in one quarter. They focused their budget on targeted social media ads and introductory offers instead of spreading resources across unrelated initiatives.

Prioritize High-ROI Channels

Not all marketing channels are created equal. Analyze which platforms offer the highest return on investment (ROI) and prioritize them in your budget allocation. Initially, this process may require experimenting with various channels. Focus your efforts on the most effective methods for engaging your target audience.

The Mitten Brewing Co. exemplifies this approach perfectly. After distributing their marketing budget across different channels, they found that community fundraising events and local tastings consistently resulted in the best customer engagement and brand loyalty.

Identifying this pattern, they revamped their marketing strategy to emphasize local initiatives, such as monthly charity collaborations and community events. Since pivoting, they've raised over $350,000 for local nonprofits and built a loyal customer base while reducing traditional advertising costs. A targeted approach is more effective than general marketing, highlighting the benefits of community-focused marketing for small craft breweries.

Leverage Data-Driven Insights

Data is a powerful ally in optimizing budget allocation. Utilize analytics to understand where your marketing spend is generating the most impact. Monitor essential metrics like customer acquisition cost (CAC), conversion rates, and lifetime value (LTV) to pinpoint efficiency gaps and areas needing improvement. Making data-driven decisions improves spending efficiency, ensuring resources target the best opportunities.

In an impressive showcase of data-driven decision-making, Plumb Works Inc., a regional plumbing company, revolutionized its marketing strategy by meticulously analyzing its customer acquisition channels.

They started by using their budget on different marketing tactics like paid search ads, social media, and email campaigns, while carefully tracking conversion rates and customer acquisition costs for each channel.

The data revealed a surprising insight: their email marketing campaigns were consistently outperforming all other channels, generating 19 tracked calls and converting 12 new customers in just one month—a 63% conversion rate.

This discovery led to reallocating the marketing budget, cutting spending on ineffective channels, and increasing investment in email marketing. The results were impressive: customer acquisition costs fell, conversion rates increased, and they achieved an ROI of $40 for every marketing dollar spent.

This strategic shift improved marketing efficiency and showed how data analytics can reveal hidden opportunities in traditional industries like plumbing, highlighting that informed decisions can significantly boost company growth.

The Targeting Snapshot

Before launching any campaign, ask:

- ⊘ Who is this for?

- ⊘ What pain are we solving?

- ⊘ Where do they live online?

- ⊘ What do they need to hear *right now*?

- ⊘ Why would they choose us over the rest?

Allocate for Flexibility

The marketing combat zone is ever-changing, and your budget should be flexible enough to adapt to new opportunities or challenges. Set aside part of your budget for experimentation and innovation to explore new strategies and adapt to market changes. This flexibility ensures that you remain agile, capable of pivoting when needed to maintain a competitive edge.

In the fiercely competitive Cincinnati home services market, Mike Silver's carpet repair business exemplifies the powerful fusion of traditional craftsmanship and cutting-edge digital innovation.

When big-box retailers relied on brand recognition, Mike's Carpet Repair in Cincinnati bet on speed. He allocated 20% of his budget to fast-cycle campaigns—blending decades of craftsmanship with modern marketing. The result? A loyal customer base, rapid growth, and a reputation that now outpaces companies 10x his size.

⚡ Speed Is Marketing Equity

In today's digital-first world, how fast you respond is part of your brand. Whether it's replying to a customer, launching a campaign, or adjusting to a trend—**speed communicates competence**.

Think of it like this: if your business takes three days to make a decision your competitor makes in three hours, you're not just slower—you *look* less confident, less capable, and less connected.

Speed doesn't just help you win—it builds trust. It tells the market: *We're paying attention. We're ready. And we're here to serve.*

Test relentlessly. Scale what works. Cut what doesn't

Continuous testing and optimization are crucial for effective budget allocation. Regularly review your campaigns, assess their performance, and refine your strategies based on insights gained. This iterative process enables you to optimize your spending, ensuring that your budget allocation consistently aligns with your strategic objectives.

Take, for example, a boutique fitness studio that implemented A/B testing across its digital campaigns. They compared various messaging and offers to find the most effective strategies for their audience, helping them adjust their budget and improve campaign results.

Consider Long-Term Investments

Although quick wins can be tempting, focusing on the long-term effects of your budget decisions is crucial. Focus your investments on strategies that cultivate sustainable growth and strengthen brand equity over the long term. Key areas to consider include content marketing, search engine optimization (SEO), and customer relationship management. These efforts may not yield immediate results, but they contribute significantly to building a strong foundation for future success.

An independent online specialty bookstore has successfully used a strong content marketing strategy that incorporates artificial intelligence (AI) for topic ideas, outlines, and SEO keywords for its copywriters. Investing in blogs and podcasts, as well as engaging with niche communities on Reddit and Quora, has helped them build a loyal customer base and enhance their brand presence. This has resulted in consistent and sustainable growth over time.

Strategic budget allocation is a disciplined approach that requires ongoing evaluation and adjustment. By understanding where to invest and where to conserve, you ensure that your marketing efforts are both efficient and effective. It's about making informed decisions that align with your objectives, maximizing the potential of every dollar spent.

When using the SMAC Framework, view your budget as a tool for strategic execution rather than just a limitation. By allocating resources wisely, you empower your brand to achieve its goals confidently and precisely. Every decision in this process influences your marketing strategy and leads your brand toward success in a competitive market.

Use these insights to effectively allocate your budget within the SMAC Framework to drive growth. Knowing where to focus your resources can effectively navigate the marketing landscape and achieve measurable results.

> *"In war, you don't waste a $100,000 missile on a $10 tent.*
> *The same goes for your budget."*

Mission III: Precision Strike Planning (Campaign Development)

Pre-launch Checklist:

🎯 **The 4Ps of Precision Campaigns**

1. **Persona** – Who's the target?

2. **Platform** – Where do they hang out?

3. **Positioning** – What are we saying?

4. **Payload** – What's the CTA or next action?

As we wrap up this chapter on precision targeting, let's summarize our insights and prepare to implement your marketing strategies. Understand your ideal customers and allocate your budget wisely, then focus on precise planning. This stage is about transforming insights into action, crafting campaigns that are not only creative but also strategically aligned with your objectives.

Recently, my agency successfully launched a unique product: medical exam gloves with an innovative doffing aid for easy removal. With a limited budget, my agency had to carefully plan and execute every marketing effort. We created a precise campaign that captured our audience's attention and surpassed expectations in engagement and sales. This experience reinforced the power of strategic planning and execution, even within constraints.

Crafting the Campaign Message

The foundation of a successful campaign lies in its message. Your message should resonate with your audience, highlight your unique value, and differentiate your brand from competitors. Craft a story that resonates with your ideal customers by tapping into their needs and desires. Use emotional language and vivid imagery to motivate them to take action.

Quinn Snacks revolutionized the natural snack category by addressing a core consumer need: the desire for complete transparency regarding the origin of their food. In an industry characterized by unclear supply chains and ambiguous sustainability claims, Quinn's founder, Kristy Lewis, boldly transformed the landscape with her groundbreaking "Farm-to-Bag" initiative, making transparency not just a buzzword but a concrete and engaging experience for consumers.

Quinn enhanced the customer experience by assigning a unique batch number to each snack bag, allowing consumers to trace the ingredients back to their origins. This initiative caters to the increasing demand for genuine food narratives. This approach appealed to conscious consumers who are skeptical of traditional marketing and seek verified proof of ethical sourcing.

The campaign was successful because it matched consumer behavior trends, with 73% of consumers willing to pay more for products that offered complete transparency. Quinn's message cut through the noise because it wasn't just making promises; it was providing proof.

The Farm-to-Bag section of their website became the second most visited area, showing how this transparency initiative turned curious visitors into engaged community members who felt connected to the farmers and processes behind their snacks. Quinn's genuine commitment to sustainability was validated with the prestigious HowGood Climate Friendly label. This shows that genuine marketing practices foster trust and loyalty that can have a lasting impact beyond the first purchase.

Selecting the Right Channels

Choosing the right channels is essential for reaching your audience effectively. Analyze where your ideal customers spend their time and how they prefer to engage with content. Choose communication channels that resonate with your audience's preferences and behaviors, whether it's social media, email, video, or events. This strategic selection ensures your message reaches them in the most powerful way possible.

The indie film *Tangerine* turned a micro-budget into a marketing asset. Shot entirely on iPhone 5s, the team leaned into the limitation—using SoundCloud tracks and social media to highlight their DIY ethos.

The result? A buzzworthy Sundance premiere, a deal with Magnolia Pictures, and $700K+ in domestic box office—all without big ad budgets. *Tangerine* proved that creativity and authenticity can outshine studio dollars.

Timing and Frequency

Timing plays a crucial role in the success of your campaigns. Determine the moments when your audience is most open to receiving your message, and strategically organize your campaign timeline to coincide with these optimal periods. Analyze seasonal trends, industry events, and consumer behaviors to find the best timing for your campaign launches.

Flying Solo transformed independent fashion retail by effectively implementing a collaborative marketing strategy tied to key industry events. This platform offers a shared-resource model that allows designers to participate in New York Fashion Week for just $6,000, rather than the usual $30,000.

Flying Solo enhanced the traditional fashion calendar by timing its shows with major fashion weeks in New York, Paris, and Milan, and coordinating seasonal launches at its SoHo and Paris boutiques for effective marketing.

Their synchronized approach to seasonal transitions and strategic press placements in publications like *Vogue* and *Harper's Bazaar* has created a sustainable ecosystem where independent designers can effectively compete with established luxury brands.

This timing strategy has made high-fashion marketing more accessible for emerging designers and has established Flying Solo as a respected platform that grabs industry attention during key fashion moments. This method not only enhanced brand awareness but also significantly drove sales during crucial shopping periods. As a result, they established a reputation for being in tune with the ever-evolving fashion landscape.

Integrating with Broader Marketing Efforts

To guarantee the success of your precision strike campaigns, it is crucial to view them not as isolated initiatives but as integral components of your comprehensive marketing strategy. This means aligning your campaigns with key initiatives such as brand awareness, customer retention, and focused product launches.

Such integration fosters a cohesive and unified approach, enhancing the overall effectiveness of your marketing efforts. It strengthens your brand message and amplifies audience engagement across various channels. Ultimately, this strategic alignment maximizes the impact of your initiatives, ensuring they effectively contribute to your long-term business goals.

Blueland has transformed eco-friendly marketing by combining targeted campaigns with a commitment to sustainability, creating a compelling story for its audience. Envision the debut of a revolutionary cleaning tablet—small, powerful, and completely waste-free—accompanied by an impactful campaign that enlightens millions on the detrimental effects of single-use plastics on our environment.

Blueland uses social media storytelling, influencer partnerships, and targeted ads to promote its products, while highlighting its commitment to sustainability and innovation. Their campaigns do more than just sell products; they ignite inspiration.

Blueland combines product launches with brand awareness and customer retention strategies, creating a cohesive message that encourages environmentally responsible purchases. This cohesive strategy has led to significant growth and established their reputation as leaders in sustainable living, demonstrating that combining precision with purpose produces game-changing results.

Monitoring and Optimization

Once your campaigns are live, continuous monitoring and optimization are crucial for maximizing effectiveness. Monitor essential key performance indicators (KPIs) to evaluate the effectiveness of your campaigns, including engagement rates, conversion metrics, and return on investment. Use these insights to refine your strategies, making data-driven adjustments that enhance campaign performance.

A regional travel agency fully embraced a data-driven approach by meticulously monitoring and evaluating its digital advertising campaigns. Through a comprehensive analysis of click-through rates and conversion data, they were able to pinpoint specific opportunities for improvement, such as refining their ad copy to be more engaging and adjusting their targeting parameters for better audience alignment.

This ongoing iterative process increased bookings and contributed to significantly stronger campaign outcomes overall. The agency's commitment to continuous improvement ultimately enhanced its overall marketing effectiveness and customer satisfaction.

Learning and Applying Insights

Each campaign provides valuable insights that are crucial for informing future strategies and enhancing overall effectiveness. Post-campaign reviews are essential for teams to identify successful elements and areas for improvement. By systematically analyzing these learnings, organizations can refine their planning and execution processes. This approach ensures each campaign improves upon previous experiences, resulting in greater success.

A healthcare provider exemplified this by analyzing the results of a patient outreach campaign. They improved their outreach strategy by analyzing patient engagement trends and preferences, leading to better patient satisfaction and care outcomes.

As we finish up this part about precision targeting, it's super important to remember that good marketing is a never-ending journey that needs regular tweaking and adapting. By refining your targeting strategies, budget allocation, and campaign planning, you position your brand for lasting success in a competitive market.

These insights prepare you for the next step of the SMAC Framework, emphasizing the importance of agility and adaptability. With a strong foundation in precise targeting, you're ready to tackle the challenges of digital marketing with strategy and creativity.

Embrace the next chapter confidently as we explore agility's power in achieving marketing excellence. Precision has laid the groundwork; now, it's time to add agility to keep your brand adaptable and prepared for opportunities and challenges.

Keep improving your strategies and execution, and follow precision targeting principles to achieve marketing mastery. The way forward is clear, the resources are available, and the possibilities are limitless. Let's move forward, transforming strategy into success and vision into reality.

Real-World Case Study: Dollar Shave Club— Precision Targeting to Disrupt the Razor Industry

In 2011, the razor aisle was dominated by major brands like Gillette and Schick, which priced their complicated products, with features like vibrating handles and multiple blades, at a premium. These Goliaths relied on flashy advertising, retail dominance, and locked-in shelf space to monopolize the market. For the average consumer, buying razors was an expensive and frustrating experience.

Then came Dollar Shave Club (DSC), a savvy start-up with a powerful vision: razors shouldn't break the bank, and getting them should be effortless. With precision targeting and a bold strategy, DSC took on the razor giants and forever changed the game.

Target Acquisition: Finding the Right Customer

Dollar Shave Club didn't try to appeal to everyone. Instead, they focused on a specific audience: men frustrated by the high prices and unnecessary features of traditional razors. These were budget-conscious, convenience-seeking customers who wanted a simple, no-frills product that worked.

DSC addressed this crucial pain point by recognizing that their target customers prioritized a quality shave over extravagant features—they simply sought an affordable, effective solution. By laser-focusing on this group, DSC avoided spreading its message too thin and captured the attention of an underserved market.

Ammunition Conservation: Making Every Dollar Count

Unlike major razor brands that invested heavily in TV ads and sponsorships, DSC operated with a limited budget. Their marketing approach was precise: to craft a single impactful piece of content that would profoundly connect with their target audience and yield the highest possible return.

That piece of content was a now-legendary launch video starring founder Michael Dubin. In the video, Dubin pitched affordable, high-quality razors delivered to your door with a mix of humor and value. With lines like "Our blades are f*ing great" and absurd gags like a forklift-driving bear, the video captured attention and sparked conversations.

Produced for just $4,500, the video went viral, racking up millions of views in a matter of days. It didn't just introduce the product—it embodied the brand's personality, speaking directly to the frustrations of its audience.

Precision Strike Planning: The Subscription Model

DSC's business model was as sharp as its razors. Rather than selling products through traditional retail channels, they opted for a subscription model. Customers can receive razors delivered to their door for a low monthly fee, avoiding the hassle of buying expensive cartridges in stores.

This model wasn't just convenient; it created recurring revenue and deepened customer loyalty. By offering multiple subscription tiers, DSC allowed customers to choose a plan that fit their needs, further reinforcing the brand's commitment to simplicity and affordability.

The David vs. Goliath Outcome

Dollar Shave Club's strategy worked. DSC hit 12,000 orders in 48 hours. Within a few years, over 3 million people subscribed—and Unilever bought the brand for $1 billion.

> *"DSC's success wasn't about outspending the giants—*
> *it was about outsmarting them."*

By understanding their audience, making every marketing dollar count, and delivering on a simple, clear value proposition, Dollar Shave Club showed how precision targeting can topple even the largest competitors.

This story is the essence of Chapter 3: when you aim with precision, you don't need a massive budget to make an industry-changing impact. Dollar Shave Club proved that the right strategy, delivered with boldness and clarity, can turn any David into a giant killer.

Chapter 3 Key Takeaways:
SHOOT—Precision Targeting

"Don't count the people you reach. Reach the people who count."
—David Ogilvy

KEY LEARNING POINTS

♦ **Why Most Businesses Fail: They Aim at the Wrong Target**

Most businesses waste money on broad, unfocused marketing campaigns. They throw their message out into the world, hoping something sticks. But **hope isn't a strategy.**

Winning businesses **target with precision,** ensuring every marketing dollar is aimed at high-value customers who are most likely to convert.

♦ **Target Acquisition: Finding Your Perfect Customer**

"Success starts with knowing exactly who you're trying to reach. If you don't have a crystal-clear understanding of your ideal customer, you're just firing blindly."

You must:

⊘ Define your **perfect** customer based on **demographics, behaviors, and motivations.**

⊘ Identify their biggest **pain points and desires**—what keeps them up at night?

⊘ Develop detailed **customer personas** that drive your messaging and campaigns.

⊘ Find where they spend time—**what platforms do they use, and how do they engage with content?**

◆ **Ammunition Conservation: Strategic Budget Allocation**

Your budget is limited, so every dollar must be spent wisely. **Random spending is just modern-day trench warfare. You'll burn through your budget before you ever reach the front line.** You need to:

- Invest in **high-ROI marketing channels** (SEO, email, social ads, etc.).
- Stop wasting money on audiences that **will never buy** from you.
- Focus on campaigns that generate **actual revenue, not vanity metrics.**
- Continuously test and refine—**double down on what works, cut what doesn't.**

◆ **Precision Strike Planning: Campaign Development**

A winning campaign is like a **military precision strike**—it's timed, targeted, and designed for maximum impact.

- **Craft a compelling message** that speaks directly to your audience's needs.
- **Select the right marketing channels** to reach them at the perfect moment.
- **Time your campaigns strategically**—seasonality and trends matter.
- **Integrate all marketing efforts** into a seamless, omnichannel experience.

◆ **The Power of Clear, Direct Messaging**

A confused prospect never buys. Your message must be:

- **Simple & clear**—no fluff, no jargon.
- **Emotional & compelling**—speak to the heart, not just the head.
- **Actionable**—tell them exactly what to do next.
- **Consistent across platforms**—your website, ads, and emails should all reinforce the same message.

◆ The War Is Won by the Businesses That Target Smarter

Most businesses waste money because they don't focus on **the right customers, the right message, and the right timing.** When you **aim with precision,** you don't need a massive budget to dominate your market.

Action Steps to Master Precision Targeting

- **Refine your customer profile**—who is your perfect customer, and where do they hang out?

- **Audit your marketing spend**—cut wasteful spending and reinvest in high-ROI channels.

- **Craft a targeted message** that speaks directly to your ideal customer's pain points.

- **Test different marketing channels** and scale the ones that perform best.

- **Eliminate vague, generic marketing**—focus on clear, compelling, and specific messaging.

Final thought: *"The businesses that win aren't the ones that market the most—they're the ones that market the smartest. Stop wasting money on the wrong people. Sharpen your aim, tighten your message, and execute with precision."*

CHAPTER 4

MOVE—Tactical Agility

"Speed is the essence of war. Take advantage of the enemy's unpreparedness; travel by unexpected routes and strike where unguarded."
—Sun Tzu, *The Art of War*

Mission Brief: CHAPTER 4 – MOVE: Tactical Agility

The battlefield shifts fast. If you can't move, you die. Agility isn't just an advantage—it's your survival instinct.

Your mission:

Outmaneuver bigger, slower competitors by reacting in real time. Learn how to test fast, pivot smart, and capitalize on momentum before it's gone. This chapter equips you with the mindset and tools to stay light on your feet and dangerous on the move.

In the chaos of battle, it's not the biggest army that wins—it's the one that moves first. In business, your ability to pivot quickly isn't a luxury—it's your strongest advantage.

The next phase of the SMAC Framework will emphasize agility, a crucial quality in today's fast-paced marketing world. Quick and strategic actions can make the difference between thriving and merely surviving for a business. This chapter shows how tactical agility helps you adapt fast and seize opportunities before your competitors do.

One of my most powerful Navy lessons came during a war game where our small ship challenged a massive carrier strike group. This was a quint-essential David and Goliath scenario, where the sheer size of our adversary appeared to give them a distinct advantage.

But our agility and ability to navigate swiftly and unpredictably allowed us to outsmart and outmaneuver the larger force. This experience highlighted an important lesson:

> *"Agility isn't just an advantage—it's necessary to outpace competitors and seize the initiative."*

In today's business world, the market is your battlefield—and the same principles apply.

> *"Unlike bigger competitors, your size is your advantage. You can move faster, adapt quicker, and strike before they even notice."*

This nimbleness enables you to pivot strategies swiftly, align with market trends, and engage with customers in real time.

Marketing agility isn't about being fast for the sake of it—it's about responding with strategy and precision. It's about having systems and processes to collect information, evaluate situations, and use resources effectively. You'll get tools to move fast, adapt faster, and keep your edge—even when the market shifts overnight.

We'll explore how speed can be your primary weapon, enabling you to outmaneuver larger competitors who are slower to react. Rapid response systems let you hit back fast when surprises happen—and act on opportunities before they disappear. Knowing your pivot points means you don't just react—you evolve with purpose.

Kitchen Fantasy, a charming specialty kitchen store nestled in the picturesque wine country of Temecula in southern California, faced an unforeseen transformation in consumer behavior as a result of the global pandemic.

After 20 years as a family-owned business, they faced bankruptcy when they had to close because they were labeled nonessential. This predicament was particularly dire given their large investment in a state-of-the-art kitchen for in-store cooking classes.

Instead of succumbing to the crisis, they quickly adapted to the trend of more people baking bread at home because of store access problems. They sourced flour and yeast from their commercial suppliers, then repackaged them into convenient portions using plastic containers from their inventory.

This decision solidified their vital role within the community, establishing them as indispensable and guaranteeing the continuity of their operations. Amidst challenges faced by larger competitors, this small store used technology effectively by hosting Facebook Live events to showcase cooking tools and new baking supplies, demonstrating how to use them for home chefs.

They introduced online cooking classes, implemented an e-commerce platform, and offered convenient curbside pickup options. Their quick adaptability kept loyal customers and attracted new ones seeking safety and convenience during uncertain times.

After the pandemic, their in-store cooking classes became very popular and sold out quickly, leveraging the customer base they had developed during that time. Ultimately, their innovative response to changing market dynamics enabled them to not just survive, but to flourish while others struggled.

This chapter urges you to view market changes as valuable opportunities rather than threats. By cultivating agility, you empower your business to navigate uncertainty with confidence, transforming potential obstacles into pathways for growth.

Prepare to explore the art of moving strategically, where every decision is informed by insights and every action is deliberate. You'll learn to adapt and succeed rapidly changing combat zones by embracing agility.

Welcome to the new battlefield, where agility and innovative tactics help you outperform your competition and achieve marketing excellence.

Speed as Your Primary Weapon

✅ A fast, imperfect move is better than a slow, perfect one.

✅ Act while others analyze.

✅ Use speed to seize the initiative and keep competitors reactive.

In the cutthroat arena of today's business world, where agility often trumps size, speed isn't just an advantage—it's your arsenal. For small to mid-sized businesses, the capacity to act quickly, decisively, and with strategic intent can be the key differentiator between being eclipsed by larger competitors and capitalizing on the opportunities they overlook.

Imagine outmaneuvering industry giants, not through brute force, but by harnessing the power of speed as your strategic asset. The MOVE concept in the SMAC Framework focuses on using quick responses and efficient execution to turn speed into a powerful advantage for your business in a rapidly changing environment.

During a joint naval exercise in the Sea of Japan, our battle group unexpectedly faced a severe storm. Surrounded by fishing vessels, we had no time for lengthy deliberations or exhaustive planning. Taking swift action was crucial. We quickly adapted our radar systems, plotted new courses, and worked together to keep our battle group safe.

This experience solidified a vital lesson: preparedness and the ability to act swiftly are crucial when confronting unexpected challenges. In marketing, this means quickly seizing opportunities and adapting to changes before others realize them.

Speed in marketing means being strategically ready to act when needed, not just acting quickly. Confidence in your knowledge, skills, and resources is crucial for making swift, informed decisions and executing effectively. This proactive approach allows you to seize trends and address challenges seamlessly. Here's how you can transform speed into your ultimate competitive advantage:

Establishing a Culture of Agility

Creating a culture that values speed and flexibility is essential for harnessing agility. This requires instilling a mindset where quick decision-making is not only accepted but celebrated. Empowering your team to make decisions, experiment, and take calculated risks without fearing failure is crucial. This cultural shift positions your organization to move swiftly and adapt seamlessly to changes as they arise.

At Everzocial, we prioritize a culture of innovation and agility through a flat organizational structure and flexible workflows.

This approach promotes open communication among all team members and reduces bureaucratic obstacles, enabling quick responses to market feedback and improving our decision-making.

We operate like a flexible team of special forces instead of a traditional army of marketers with strict hierarchies. This approach enables us to stay sharply focused and agile in turbulent terrain. This model is crucial for collaborating with small to mid-sized businesses seeking rapid growth, as it helps us effectively support our clients in reaching their ambitious goals.

Implementing Agile Processes

Agile methodologies are remarkably effective for achieving rapid and efficient outcomes. Consider implementing proven project management strategies such as Agile and Scrum, which emphasize incremental progress and adaptability.

These approaches enable teams to address tasks in short sprints while adjusting based on real-time feedback. By embracing these methodologies, your organization can enhance its ability to pivot swiftly and deliver results with precision.

In a remarkable display of agile transformation, Healthfirst emerged as a pioneering force in healthcare technology by revolutionizing its development approach through agile AI/ML implementation. Starting in 2019, this innovative yet lesser-known healthcare organization demonstrated how breaking down complex healthcare challenges into manageable sprints could yield extraordinary results.

Through their disciplined application of agile methodologies, Healthfirst successfully developed and deployed an impressive array of 978 custom features and 17 predictive models, while seamlessly integrating 612 pre-built templates into their healthcare delivery system.

Their iterative approach accelerated their development cycle and ensured that each solution was thoroughly tested and validated before reaching their 1.7 million members. This systematic transformation showcases how a healthcare organization can successfully balance rapid technological advancement with the critical need for accuracy and reliability in patient care.

Leveraging Technology

Technology is a powerful enabler of speed and agility. Utilize tools and platforms that enhance communication, collaboration, and data analysis. Automation, in particular, can streamline repetitive tasks, freeing time for strategic thinking and creative problem-solving. By harnessing technology, you equip your team with the resources needed to act swiftly and decisively.

Hosanna Revival, a Bible e-commerce store, improved its customer service by using AI chatbots to increase efficiency and enhance the customer experience. These chatbots quickly and effectively handled routine inquiries, such as order statuses and product availability, drastically reducing response times. The automation increased customer satisfaction and enabled the company to resolve common questions more quickly, creating a better experience for its expanding customer base.

Hosanna Revival automated repetitive tasks, allowing its team to focus on complex issues and provide personalized customer care. Balancing technology with human expertise improved the service experience, allowing the company to retain a personal touch while expanding operations. Hosanna Revival has become a leader in its niche by using automation to maintain competitiveness and provide excellent service.

Developing Rapid Response Protocols

Okay, so you know how sometimes things just *happen* in business? A customer has a meltdown on social media, a crisis occurs, or you urgently need to release a new promotion. Yeah, those moments.

This is where being prepared isn't just a good idea, it's *everything*. We're talking about having solid, rapid-response plans in place. Think of them as your "What to Do When Things Go Sideways (or Suddenly Get Really Exciting)" guide.

Basically, you need clearly defined steps for different situations. What's the plan if a customer lodges a serious complaint? Who handles it, what are the steps, and how quickly should they respond? The same goes for more significant crises—having a predetermined protocol cuts down on the frantic scrambling and lets everyone know their role. Even something positive, like needing a lightning-fast marketing push, benefits from a plan.

Why is all this preplanning so crucial? Because it saves precious time. When the clock is ticking, you don't want your team stuck in a meeting room debating the best course of action. You want them *acting*. Having those rapid response protocols in place means less deliberation and more *doing*. Everyone already knows the drill.

It's not just about speed. It's about confidence. When your team knows there's a plan, they feel more empowered to handle whatever comes their way. They're not starting from scratch every time; they have a framework, a roadmap to follow.

This translates to a better experience for everyone. Customers see that you're on top of things, even when things get tricky. Your team feels less stressed and more in control. And your business can adapt to changes (both good and bad) with a lot more grace and efficiency.

So, take the time to think through those "what if" scenarios and build rapid-response protocols. It's an investment that pays off big time when you need it most! It will transform the company's capacity to handle unexpected issues.

An excellent example of an effective rapid-response protocol comes from a regional airline during an unexpected travel surge. By implementing well-defined plans for resource reallocation and schedule adjustments, they swiftly adapted to the increased demand. This proactive approach not only ensured smooth operations without sacrificing service quality, but also strengthened customer trust and loyalty.

Agility Readiness Checklist

✅ Can your team make same-day marketing decisions?

✅ Do you monitor market signals weekly (not quarterly)?

✅ Can you launch a test campaign in under 48 hours?

✅ Are your internal approvals faster than your competition?

If you answered "no" to any, your agility is costing you customers.

Monitoring Market Trends

To act quickly, you must be aware of what's happening in the market, and implement systems for monitoring industry trends, competitor activities, and consumer behavior. By staying informed, you identify opportunities and threats as they arise, positioning your business to respond with agility.

It's always inspiring to see how agility and strategic market awareness can shape the trajectory of a business. A remarkable example is a small beverage company that showcased outstanding foresight by keenly monitoring and adapting to emerging health trends in its industry. Recognizing a steady shift in consumer preferences toward natural hydration options, the company didn't hesitate to act. They created and launched a line of organic beverages to meet the growing demand for healthier, all-natural options.

This quick and intentional move appealed to health-conscious consumers and helped the brand stand out in a competitive market. Their ability to monitor trends, adapt quickly, and offer innovative products led to significant sales growth. This example shows how businesses of any size can use timely insights to gain momentum and create lasting effects.

Encouraging Continuous Learning

Speed requires the ability to learn and adapt on the fly. To stay ahead of the competition, your organization must master the art of learning and adapting swiftly. Imagine a workplace where continuous learning isn't just encouraged—it's celebrated.

When your team members are empowered to acquire new skills and knowledge, your organization transforms into a dynamic force, poised to pivot seamlessly as new strategies and technologies emerge. Promoting a culture of lifelong learning keeps your operations flexible and encourages innovation and resilience in your employees.

Investing in growth creates a proactive workforce ready to handle any challenge. So let's prioritize learning today, and watch your organization thrive tomorrow.

A healthcare provider embraced this approach by offering ongoing training and development opportunities for staff. By encouraging continuous learning, they stayed ahead of medical advancements and regulatory changes, enhancing patient care and organizational resilience.

Speed as a primary weapon is not about rushing recklessly; it's about combining preparedness with decisive action. The goal is to create an environment where your team is prepared to act and has the right tools to do so effectively. By leveraging speed, you gain the upper hand in a competitive landscape, turning agility into a strategic advantage.

As we move forward in exploring the SMAC Framework, remember that speed is not just a tactic—it's a mindset. It's about being ready to adapt, innovate, and execute, ensuring that your business remains relevant and competitive. Harnessing speed helps you confidently navigate market complexities, turning challenges into opportunities for lasting success.

Leverage speed in the SMAC Framework to boost your strategic execution and achieve meaningful results. You control the path to agility, guiding your brand toward its goals and securing its position in the market.

Rapid Response Protocols

Rapid Response Playbook

- React to competitor moves within 24 hours
- Adjust messaging within days, not weeks
- Re-launch failed campaigns fast with new learnings

As a Petty Officer Second Class in the Combat Information Center during the Cold War, I learned that hesitation can be deadly. Our success relied on quick decisions supported by strong protocols, whether tracking radar blips or adapting to sudden changes. Today's digital marketing landscape isn't so different from those tense moments in the CIC.

I vividly recall a midnight watch when a series of unexpected radar contacts appeared out of nowhere, requiring urgent classification and action. Our team's ability to execute predetermined protocols without missing a beat was the difference between mission success and failure.

Similarly, in today's marketing battles, your team's capacity to pivot and respond to market shifts, competitor moves, or viral trends can make or break your campaign.

Think of your rapid response protocols as your marketing battle stations. Just as we had clearly defined roles and response patterns for every possible scenario at sea, your marketing team needs established frameworks for common digital challenges. Sudden market shifts. Competitor launches. Social media crises. Technical failures. Viral opportunities. The key isn't just speed—it's coordinated, purposeful action.

We never just reacted in the CIC; we responded according to well-rehearsed protocols that we practiced over and over again. Your marketing team needs the same level of preparation and clarity.

Remember: In both naval operations and digital marketing, victory doesn't go to the biggest player, but to the one who can adapt and respond most effectively. Establish your protocols now, drill them regularly, and stay ready. Because in this digital age, just like in the CIC, opportunity strikes without warning.

The seas of digital marketing may be different from the Cold War waters I patrolled, but the principles remain the same: Clear protocols, practiced responses, and a team ready to execute at a moment's notice.

When it is time for battle stations, is your marketing team ready to respond? Here's how to develop and implement these protocols in your marketing strategy:

Anticipate Scenarios

Start by identifying potential scenarios that could impact your marketing efforts. These might include changes in consumer behavior, new competitive threats, or shifts in regulatory environments. By anticipating these scenarios, you can develop tailored response plans that address specific challenges and opportunities.

In a remarkable display of crisis management excellence, Buffer's handling of its 2013 security breach stands as a masterclass in organizational preparedness and authentic leadership during turbulent times.

When faced with a security incident affecting 30,000 users on a quiet Saturday afternoon, Buffer's response transformed what could have been a catastrophic blow to their reputation into a testament to their organizational integrity. Within mere minutes of detecting unauthorized access, their pre-established crisis protocols kicked into action, demonstrating the immense value of having robust response mechanisms in place before disaster strikes.

Rather than retreating into damage control mode, Buffer took the bold step of immediate transparency, notifying users about the breach even before they had fully assessed its scope—a decision that would later prove pivotal in maintaining customer trust. Their multi-channel communication strategy unfolded with precision, combining direct email notifications, real-time social media updates, and comprehensive security status reports, all while their technical team worked tirelessly to implement enhanced encryption measures.

This proactive approach not only minimized the breach's impact but actually strengthened Buffer's market position, as customers witnessed firsthand the company's unwavering commitment to their security and trust. The incident transformed from a potential crisis into a powerful demonstration of how thorough preparation, swift action, and transparent communication can preserve and enhance a company's reputation in the face of adversity.

Define Roles and Responsibilities

Clarity is key to effective execution. Establish clear roles and responsibilities for your team members during a rapid response. Ensure everyone knows their part in the plan, from decision-makers to those executing specific tasks. This clarity reduces confusion and streamlines action, allowing your team to respond cohesively and efficiently.

A regional restaurant chain faced a significant challenge when new health codes were unexpectedly revised, potentially disrupting operations. They responded strategically by clearly assigning roles to team members, including communication leaders and compliance officers. This proactive approach enabled them to navigate the complexities of the new regulations swiftly and efficiently.

As a result, they adapted quickly, maintained seamless operations, and preserved customer confidence during a potentially turbulent period. Their success highlights the importance of teamwork, clear roles, and a proactive approach in achieving compliance and maintaining business continuity amid changing regulations.

Develop Actionable Plans

For every scenario identified, developing a comprehensive action plan that explicitly details the specific steps required for effective response is imperative. The plans must be detailed and actionable, outlining specific actions, timelines, and responsible individuals or teams for each step.

Additionally, it's important to incorporate decision-making criteria that guide the response, establish communication protocols to ensure everyone is informed and aligned, and formulate contingency plans to address potential unforeseen circumstances, ensuring that the response is comprehensive and effective. Doing so will create a robust framework that enhances preparedness and facilitates prompt, organized action in any situation.

Establish Communication Channels

Effective communication is the cornerstone of any rapid response endeavor, significantly influencing the outcome. It is essential to establish distinct and reliable channels for both internal and external communication, ensuring that information flows smoothly and accurately among all parties involved. This structured approach should include the preparation of preapproved messaging templates and comprehensive communication guidelines, which are vital for maintaining consistency and coherence throughout the response process. By implementing these strategies, organizations can enhance their ability to communicate effectively and respond swiftly to any situation.

A healthcare provider showed dedication to handling patient inquiries during a health crisis by creating a centralized communication hub. This initiative streamlined patient interactions, ensuring timely and consistent responses aligned with current health guidelines.

Consequently, this approach significantly contributed to building trust with patients while improving the clarity of the information shared. Ultimately, it showcases the importance of transparent communication during health emergencies.

Implement Monitoring Systems

To respond swiftly and effectively, you must remain updated on the evolving changes within your surrounding market environment. This necessitates deploying advanced monitoring systems capable of providing real-time insights into critical areas, including market dynamics, changes in consumer sentiment, and competitor activities.

These systems help you spot emerging trends and potential challenges early, giving you the time to respond effectively. Ultimately, this proactive approach empowers you to navigate the fast-paced landscape with agility and foresight.

During the recent economic downturn, while competitors were flying blind, this specialty travel agency was picking up crucial signals. Their monitoring systems identified early indicators of changing travel trends: a rise in domestic bookings, a heightened demand for flexible cancellation policies, and an increasing interest in destinations suitable for remote work.

But here's where it gets interesting: They didn't just gather data; they acted on it. Within weeks, they revamped their vacation packages to focus on domestic destinations, introduced more flexible booking terms, and created new "workcation" packages for digital nomads. The result? While other travel businesses struggled, this agency kept strong customer relationships and gained market share from less adaptable competitors.

The key lesson? In today's fast-moving business environment, implementing robust monitoring systems isn't just about keeping track—it's about staying ahead. Your customers are telling you what they want. Are you equipped to listen?

Regularly Review and Update Protocols

The market is dynamic, and your response plans must evolve accordingly. Regularly review and update your rapid response protocols to ensure they remain relevant and effective. Incorporate lessons learned from past responses and adapt to changes in your business environment.

Successful organizations understand that protocols are living documents, not static relics gathering dust in a corporate manual. A leading financial services firm revamped its crisis management from a reactive approach to a proactive, flexible system.

By conducting quarterly systematic reviews of its crisis management protocols, this organization showcased its dedication to continuous improvement and achieving operational excellence. These regular assessments were not just bureaucratic tasks but valuable chances to gain real-world insights, learn from past experiences, and prepare for future challenges.

Foster a Culture of Readiness

A culture of readiness is essential for effective rapid response. Encourage a mindset where team members are vigilant, informed, and prepared to act. Provide training and simulations to reinforce protocols and build confidence in the response process, ensuring your organization is poised to tackle challenges head-on.

An energy company embraced this culture by conducting regular emergency drills and cross-functional workshops. These initiatives cultivated a proactive and prepared workforce capable of managing unexpected events with agility and assurance.

Rapid response protocols are not just about reacting; they're about responding smartly and strategically. Implementing these protocols enables your business to tackle uncertainty with confidence, turning potential challenges into valuable opportunities for growth and innovation.

As we continue exploring the SMAC Framework, remember that rapid response is crucial to agility. It's about being flexible and adapting your marketing to stay relevant and effective in a changing world. Clear protocols boost your confidence to tackle challenges and direct your brand toward successful outcomes.

Use these insights to enhance your approach in the SMAC Framework, making quick responses a key part of your strategy. By embracing agility, you can navigate market complexities with foresight and flexibility, helping your brand thrive amidst change.

Strategic Pivot Points

> If you're not already planning your next move, you're falling behind. The battlefield shifts daily—wait too long, and someone faster will take your position.

As we wrap up our exploration of agility within the SMAC Framework, it is time to consolidate the insights we've gathered and set the stage for strategic pivot points. This final piece of the agility puzzle is about cultivating the ability to change course with purpose and precision, ensuring that your business remains aligned with market dynamics and consumer demands.

Reflecting on my experiences, a particular scenario in a wargame exercise illustrates the essence of strategic pivoting. We were tasked with simulating an engagement against a larger naval force. Initially, our strategies seemed sound, but as the exercise unfolded, the situation demanded an unexpected pivot. By quickly reassessing the landscape and adjusting our tactics, we managed to outmaneuver the simulated adversary. This experience under-scored a critical lesson: the ability to pivot strategically is not just about reacting—it's about transforming challenges into opportunities.

In the business world, strategic pivot points are the moments when a shift in strategy can redefine your trajectory. It's about recognizing when to change direction and doing so with calculated intent. Here's how you can cultivate the ability to pivot strategically, ensuring that your business remains agile and competitive:

Cultivate Strategic Awareness

The foundation of effective pivoting is awareness. Encourage a mindset attuned to market changes, consumer trends, and emerging opportunities. This involves staying informed through continuous learning, industry networking, and competitive analysis. By cultivating strategic awareness, you equip your team with the insights to anticipate shifts and act accord-ingly.

As a business leader, staying ahead of the curve requires cultivating strategic awareness. Let's take the example of a tech start-up that prior-itized this. They didn't just sit back and wait for change to happen; they actively sought out industry thought leaders, attended conferences, and kept a close eye on the latest technological advancements. They noticed a rapidly growing trend in automation affecting various sectors.

> *"Winning businesses don't get stuck in outdated strategies.*
> *They know when to pivot—and they do it quickly."*

This foresight gave them the agility to pivot their product development focus to meet the rising demand for automation solutions. As a result, they not only elevated their product game but also secured a competitive edge in the market. By being proactive and adaptable, they set themselves up for long-term success in an ever-changing industry landscape.

The key takeaway is that cultivating strategic awareness is not just about staying informed—it's about using that knowledge to drive informed decisions and stay ahead of the competition. By adopting this mindset, you can position your business for success in even the most dynamic markets.

Embrace a Flexible Mindset

Flexibility is key to executing a successful pivot. Encourage a culture that values adaptability and open-mindedness, where team members are willing to explore new ideas and approaches. This mindset fosters innovation and creativity, enabling your organization to pivot with agility and confidence.

Take, for example, a boutique interior design studio that turned adaptability into its core strength. This creative team encouraged experimentation, allowing designers to challenge norms and rethink traditional methods. The studio encouraged its team to experiment with bold colors, unique layouts, and unexpected material combinations.

This openness to innovation didn't only fuel creativity—it gave the business a competitive edge. By consistently delivering fresh, imaginative solutions, the studio became known for its ability to tailor designs to clients' evolving preferences. When trends shifted or a client's needs changed mid-project, the team was already in a position to pivot seamlessly. Their flexibility and open-mindedness improved their work and built trust with clients, demonstrating their commitment to originality and adaptability.

This example underscores a powerful truth: a flexible mindset turns challenges into opportunities. Empowering your team to experiment and embrace change makes your business resilient rather than reactive.

Identify Trigger Points

Trigger points are the indicators that signal the need for a strategic pivot. These might include changes in consumer behavior, industry disruptions, or shifts in competitive positioning. By identifying and monitoring these trigger points, you can anticipate when a pivot is necessary and prepare to act decisively.

A regional retailer successfully identified a trigger point when they noticed a significant increase in online shopping. They enhanced their e-commerce platform and provided exclusive online promotions to attract new customers and support growth in response to the challenges faced by their physical stores.

Develop a Pivot Framework

A structured framework for pivoting provides the guidance needed to execute strategic changes effectively. This framework should outline the decision-making process, criteria for evaluating pivot options, and steps for implementation. Having a clear framework in place ensures that pivots are well-considered and executed with precision.

A healthcare provider created a comprehensive pivot framework featuring specific criteria for evaluating new service offerings and a strategic roadmap for seamlessly integrating these services into its current portfolio. This framework enabled them to pivot strategically in response to regulatory changes, maintaining service continuity and patient satisfaction.

Engage Stakeholders

Engaging stakeholders is crucial for successful pivot execution. Communicate transparently with team members, partners, and customers, ensuring everyone aligns with the new direction. By fostering collaboration and buy-in, you create a unified effort toward achieving the objectives of the pivot.

A nonprofit organization demonstrated this principle by engaging donors and volunteers in its strategic pivot toward digital fundraising. Through open communication and collaborative planning, they successfully transitioned their efforts online, resulting in increased support and community engagement.

Test and Iterate

Before fully committing to a pivot, consider testing new strategies on a smaller scale. This allows you to assess feasibility, identify potential challenges, and refine your approach before deploying it broadly. By iterating based on real-world feedback, you increase the likelihood of a successful pivot.

A boutique skincare brand embraced this approach by piloting a subscription model for its products. They tested the concept with a select group of customers, improved it based on feedback, and successfully launched it, boosting customer loyalty and revenue.

Measure and Learn

After executing a pivot, measure the outcomes and evaluate the impact on your business objectives. Analyze key performance metrics and gather feedback from stakeholders to assess the effectiveness of the pivot. Use these insights to inform future strategies and ensure continuous improvement.

A financial services firm exemplified this by conducting post-pivot reviews to assess the success of its digital transformation efforts. By analyzing customer feedback and operational performance, they identified areas for further optimization, ensuring sustained success and adaptability.

As we conclude this chapter on agility, remember that strategic pivoting is about more than just change—it's about deliberate evolution. By embracing agility and cultivating the ability to pivot strategically, you position your business to navigate uncertainty with confidence and resilience.

This chapter prepares you for the next phase of the SMAC Framework, focusing on adaptability as the key to your strategy. Embracing agility allows you to turn challenges into opportunities and guide your brand to lasting success in a changing market.

Use these insights to enhance your progress within the SMAC Framework, making agility a key factor in driving growth and innovation. By strategically pivoting, you can navigate market complexities with foresight and flexibility, helping your brand succeed in a changing environment.

"The businesses that win are not the biggest—they are the fastest."

Real-World Case Study: Netflix—Tactical Agility to Dominate the Entertainment Industry

In the late 1990s, the home entertainment industry was dominated by Goliaths like Blockbuster. Renting a movie meant driving to a store, hoping your choice was in stock, and paying hefty late fees if you didn't return it on time. Netflix, a scrappy start-up founded in 1997 by Reed Hastings and Marc Randolph, entered the scene with a bold idea: offer DVDs by mail with no late fees.

It was an innovative model, but their real story of dominance came later, when their ability to move fast, adjust to market signals, and embrace new technology turned them into the undisputed king of streaming.

Speed as a Weapon

Netflix's first move was to disrupt Blockbuster's rental model with its subscription-based DVD-by-mail service. For a monthly fee, customers could rent as many DVDs as they wanted, delivered straight to their door, with no due dates or late fees. This speed to market allowed Netflix to gain traction among consumers frustrated with the inefficiencies of traditional rental stores.

In 2000, Netflix approached Blockbuster with an offer to sell its business for $50 million. Blockbuster declined, dismissing Netflix as a niche player. This rejection ignited Netflix's drive to move even faster and outmaneuver its much larger rival.

Rapid Response to Market Signals

By the early 2000s, it was clear that physical DVDs would eventually give way to digital streaming as internet speeds improved. Netflix didn't wait—they moved first. While others watched the shift, they became the shift. In 2007, Netflix pivoted, launching its streaming service years ahead of major competitors.

Rather than relying solely on DVDs, Netflix began licensing movies and TV shows for digital streaming. This pivot wasn't just bold; it was pivotal. While Blockbuster was doubling down on brick-and-mortar stores, Netflix responded to market signals. It shifted its entire business model, setting the stage for a new era of entertainment consumption.

Strategic Pivot Points: Investing in Original Content

By the early 2010s, Netflix recognized that relying solely on licensed content from studios left it vulnerable to losing key titles to competitors. They moved swiftly to address this vulnerability by producing their own original content.

In 2013, Netflix released *House of Cards*, its first major original series. It was a risk, but it paid off—*House of Cards* received critical acclaim and demonstrated Netflix's ability to compete with traditional studios.

This move marked a strategic pivot from being just a content distributor to becoming a content creator. Netflix continued to double down, producing blockbuster hits like *Stranger Things*, *The Crown*, and *The Witcher*.

Today, Netflix's library of original content is one of its most significant competitive advantages, attracting subscribers globally and differentiating it from rivals like Hulu, Amazon Prime, and Disney+.

Embracing New Technology

Netflix's success also hinged on its ability to leverage emerging technology to deliver a superior user experience. From developing advanced algorithms for personalized recommendations to optimizing streaming quality for different internet speeds, Netflix consistently stayed ahead of the curve.

The company also adopted a global mindset, expanding its streaming services internationally and creating localized content to appeal to diverse audiences. This technological and cultural agility allowed Netflix to scale rapidly and dominate markets far beyond its U.S. origins.

The Outcome: A New Industry Leader

Today, Netflix is the world's leading streaming platform, with over 230 million subscribers in 190 countries. Their ability to move fast, adapt to new realities, and embrace innovation allowed them to topple Blockbuster and redefine how the world consumes entertainment.

Netflix's story exemplifies the principles in Chapter 4: Agility is the ultimate weapon. By acting quickly, anticipating change, and pivoting when necessary, Netflix proved that even a small player can outmaneuver industry giants.

Their success wasn't about brute force—it was about speed, strategy, and the willingness to embrace the future. For businesses navigating rapid change, Netflix is the ultimate example of how tactical agility can transform a David into a dominant force.

Chapter 4 Key Takeaways:
MOVE—Tactical Agility

"Agility isn't a tactic—it's a weapon. Your speed is your unfair advantage when the market hesitates."
—Kevin McGrew

KEY LEARNING POINTS

♦ Why Agility Beats Size in Marketing

Big companies have big budgets but also move **slowly**—bogged down by layers of approval, rigid strategies, and bureaucratic inertia. **Your advantage? Speed.**

Smaller, more agile businesses **pivot faster, react quicker, and capitalize on opportunities before corporate giants notice them.**

♦ Speed as Your Primary Weapon

The faster you act, the more opportunities you can seize before competitors react.

- **Test ideas rapidly.** Don't wait for perfection—get into the market and adjust based on real feedback.

- **Make quick decisions.** Speed trumps hesitation. A fast, imperfect move is better than a slow, perfect one.

- **Capitalize on trends immediately.** If you see an opportunity, jump on it before competitors do.

- **Avoid analysis paralysis.** Overthinking kills momentum—trust your data and instincts.

♦ Rapid Response Protocols: Be Ready for Anything

Just like in military operations, your business needs **protocols for rapid execution.** These systems help you **respond to crises, capitalize on emerging trends, and adjust campaigns on the fly.**

- **Competitor moves?** Be ready to counter within 24 hours.

- **Industry shifts?** Adjust messaging and offerings within days, not weeks.

- **Viral trends?** Engage while they're hot—waiting too long kills opportunity.

- **Marketing failure?** Quickly analyze, adapt, and relaunch stronger.

◆ **Strategic Pivot Points: Knowing When to Shift**

- If **customer behavior shifts**, adapt your product or service.

- If **a marketing channel underperforms**, reallocate the budget immediately.

- If **competitors copy your strategy**, find a new angle before they catch up.

- If **a trend emerges**, leverage it before the market gets saturated.

◆ **How Tactical Agility Wins Market Share**

A small business **can outmaneuver corporate competitors** by:

- **Being first to market** with new offers, promotions, and product adjustments.

- **Shifting ad spend quickly** based on real-time performance data.

- **Leveraging social media trends** in real time instead of waiting for approval.

- **Launching products faster** without excessive testing delays.

◆ **The War Is Won by the Businesses That Move First**

Marketing warfare is all about speed. Slow businesses get left behind. The winners are the ones that:

- **React to opportunities before the competition does.**

- **Make decisions in hours, not weeks.**

- **Test new approaches quickly and refine on the go.**

- **Ditch failing strategies fast and pivot to what works.**

Action Steps to Master Tactical Agility

- **Review your marketing processes.** Where are you too slow? Where can you act faster?

- **Set up rapid response protocols**—be ready to react to competitor moves, trends, and market shifts.

- **Trim unnecessary approvals**—if decisions take too long, remove bottlenecks.

- **Test and iterate faster**—launch small, analyze results, and scale what works.

- **Identify key pivot points**—know when to shift strategies before it's too late.

Final thought: *"The businesses that win don't move the most—they move first. Speed is your weapon. Agility is your edge. Use them both. Stop overanalyzing, stop waiting for perfection, and start executing with speed, strategy, and agility."*

CHAPTER 5

ADAPT—Combat Evolution

"The measure of intelligence is the ability to change."
—Albert Einstein

Mission Brief: CHAPTER 5 – ADAPT: Combat Evolution

No plan survives first contact with the market. The brands that win aren't the ones with perfect strategies—they're the ones that evolve under fire.

Your mission:

Build a business that learns, adjusts, and thrives in uncertainty. This chapter shows you how to assess what's working, fix what's not, and turn feedback into fuel. Because in this war, the most adaptable force wins.

We've moved. Now we must evolve. This stage of the SMAC Framework is all about adaptation.

"While agility allows you to maneuver quickly, adaptability ensures you remain relevant and effective in a landscape of constant change."

◆ **Agility** is how fast you move.

◆ **Adaptability** is whether you're moving in the *right direction*.

In this chapter, we'll break down how to evolve your strategy by building intelligence systems that help you pivot ahead of the curve—not behind it.

One of my sharpest memories is of a sudden storm that caught our ship off guard at sea. The storm was relentless, demanding immediate adaptation of our radar systems and navigation strategies. Instead of resisting, we shifted course and turned the storm's force into fuel.

"This ability to adapt—rather than resist—taught us an invaluable lesson about embracing change to ensure survival and success."

In marketing, adaptation isn't just reacting—it's anticipating. It means building systems that track customer behavior, tech trends, and competitor moves in real time—and convert those insights into strategy. This chapter shows you how to do exactly that so you can pivot before the market forces you to.

We'll explore the importance of intelligence-gathering systems, which are the foundation for informed decision-making. These systems reveal trends, customer patterns, and competitor movements—all essential to your next strategic move. By leveraging these insights, you can refine your strategies, ensuring they remain relevant and impactful.

One mid-sized e-commerce brand I worked with was under pressure from better-funded competitors. Instead of panicking, they doubled down on data—tracking preferences, behaviors, and gaps. That insight led them to launch hyper-personalized shopping experiences, and within six months, they were outperforming brands 10x their size.

This chapter invites you to embrace the fluidity of the market, recognizing that change is not a disruption but an opportunity for growth. By fostering adaptability, you empower your business to navigate uncertainty with confidence, transforming potential obstacles into pathways for innovation and success.

Prepare to explore the art of strategic adaptation, where every decision is informed by insights and every action is deliberate. With adaptability as your guiding principle, you'll master the ability to evolve, thrive, and lead in a marketplace where the only constant is change. Welcome to a world where insight and strategy converge, equipping you with the tools to adapt and excel in the dynamic landscape of digital marketing.

Intelligence-Gathering Systems

In the ever-shifting landscape of digital marketing, intelligence is your guiding light, illuminating the path toward informed adaptation. The ability to gather, analyze, and apply insights sets the foundation for strategic evolution in a market where change is the only constant. This section explores the creation and implementation of intelligence-gathering systems—tools and processes that empower you to convert raw data into actionable strategies.

Reflecting on my early naval experiences, I recall a night operation where intelligence was our greatest asset. We relied on a network of sensors and signals, weaving together seemingly disparate data points to form a cohesive picture of our surroundings. Each blip on the radar and each subtle shift in the water contributed to our understanding, enabling us to make decisions with precision and confidence. In marketing, this same principle applies: informed intelligence allows you to see the full landscape and act with strategic clarity.

Building intelligence-gathering systems is about creating a robust infrastructure that captures valuable data and translates it into insights. Here's how you can establish these systems effectively, ensuring that your business remains adaptable and informed:

Identify Key Data Sources

The first step in building an intelligence system is identifying the key data sources relevant to your business. This includes internal data like sales reports, customer feedback, and web analytics, as well as external data such as industry trends, competitor activities, and social media sentiment. By pinpointing these sources, you lay the groundwork for a comprehensive understanding of the market environment.

For example, a regional furniture retailer identified key data sources by integrating point-of-sale systems with online analytics. This approach provided a holistic view of customer purchasing behaviors, allowing the business to tailor its offerings and marketing strategies to better meet consumer needs.

Implement Data Collection Tools

Utilize tools and technologies that facilitate efficient data collection. These may include CRM systems, analytics platforms, and social listening tools. By implementing these technologies, you automate the data collection process, ensuring that your intelligence system is both efficient and scalable.

Consider a digital marketing agency that implemented a combination of CRM and social listening tools. This integration allowed them to track client interactions, monitor brand mentions, and gather real-time feedback, which provided ongoing insights to shape their campaign strategies.

Analyze Data for Insights

Raw data is only as valuable as the insights it produces. Implement analytical processes that transform data into meaningful information. This involves using data analysis techniques like segmentation, trend analysis, and predictive modeling to identify patterns and insights that support informed decision-making.

A SaaS start-up utilized advanced analytics to segment its user base and analyze engagement patterns. By focusing on the features users engaged with the most, they prioritized product enhancements, boosting user satisfaction and retention.

Create Actionable Dashboards

Developing dashboards that effectively visualize data is essential for presenting information in a clear and actionable manner. These dashboards should not only highlight critical metrics and emerging trends but also provide stakeholders with an at-a-glance overview of overall performance, making it easier for them to grasp essential insights quickly.

By ensuring data is both accessible and easily understandable, you empower teams to engage in informed discussions and drive strategic planning initiatives effectively. Ultimately, well-designed dashboards serve as valuable tools for making data-driven decisions within the organization.

A healthcare provider demonstrated this by creating dashboards that tracked patient engagement and satisfaction metrics. These visualizations provided insights into service performance and patient needs, guiding improvements in care delivery and patient communication.

Establish Feedback Loops

Feedback loops play a crucial role in the continuous improvement of insights, ensuring that they are not only accurate but also relevant over time. It is important to establish structured processes for collecting and integrating feedback from diverse sources, including customers, employees, and partners, as this can provide a comprehensive view of needs and expectations.

By nurturing this ongoing dialogue, organizations can effectively refine their intelligence systems, leading to more informed decisions and strategies that reflect real-world experiences and perspectives. Embracing feedback in this way ultimately enhances the significantly improved responsiveness of the organization in a rapidly changing environment.

Nordstrom, a prominent retail chain, used this approach by consistently implementing regular customer surveys and structured employee feedback sessions, creating a robust system for gathering insights. These feedback loops revealed valuable insights into operational efficiencies and shed light on customer preferences, which are crucial for tailored service.

As a result, the business was able to drive continuous improvement and foster innovation, enhancing its overall performance in a competitive market. By actively engaging both customers and employees in this way, the retailer effectively adapted to changing demands and significantly improved its offerings.

Foster a Data-Driven Culture

Creating an intelligence system is not just about technology; it's about fostering a culture that values data-driven decision-making. Encourage team members to engage with data, ask questions, and explore insights. By embedding this culture within your organization, you empower your team to leverage intelligence in their daily operations, driving strategic alignment and innovation.

A financial services firm embraced this culture by hosting regular data workshops and training sessions. These initiatives equipped employees with the skills and confidence to analyze data, fostering a company-wide commitment to data-driven strategies and intelligent decision-making.

Adapt and Iterate

The intelligence system you build today must be adaptable to future changes. Regularly review and update your data sources, tools, and analytical processes to ensure they remain relevant and effective. Strategic adaptation is driven by actionable insights. These insights are provided by an intelligence system that is maintained and improved through iteration.

An e-commerce brand demonstrated this by regularly updating its intelligence system with new data sources and analytical tools. This iterative approach ensured that their marketing strategies remained aligned with evolving consumer preferences and competitive dynamics.

Establishing robust intelligence-gathering systems will equip your business with the insights needed to adapt and thrive in a dynamic market. These systems transform data into a strategic asset, guiding your decisions and actions with clarity and confidence.

As we move forward in exploring the SMAC Framework, remember that intelligence is not just about collecting data—it's about unlocking insights that drive adaptation and innovation. With a comprehensive understanding of your market, you are prepared to navigate change with agility, ensuring that your business remains relevant and competitive.

Prepare to leverage these insights as you advance through the SMAC Framework, turning intelligence into a powerful driver of strategic execution. With adaptability as your guiding principle, you navigate the complexities of the market with foresight and flexibility, ensuring your brand thrives amidst the shifting landscape.

Battle Damage Assessment (Analytics & Optimization)

To adapt effectively, the next important step is to conduct a battle damage assessment, which involves evaluating how well your marketing strategies and campaigns are working. It's not just about counting successes and failures; it's about learning from every action. Each campaign, successful or not, should help you grow and evolve.

Based on my naval experience, evaluating the outcome of an engagement is just as important as the engagement itself. Once the dust settled, we meticulously reviewed every maneuver, every decision, and every outcome. By doing so, we identified what worked and what needed adjustment, refining our strategies for future missions. In marketing, this post-campaign analysis is your opportunity to learn and adapt, transforming data into a roadmap for continuous improvement.

To effectively assess battle damage, follow these steps to maximize insights from your campaign experiences:

1. Define Success Metrics

Before launching any campaign, establish clear success metrics that align with your strategic objectives. These metrics serve as benchmarks for evaluating performance, guiding your analysis of what constitutes success. Defining metrics like brand awareness, lead generation, and sales conversions from the start keeps your assessment focused and relevant.

Take, for example, a regional tourism board that proactively launched a comprehensive campaign to boost off-season travel to its area. They've established a structured framework by defining metrics like website traffic, booking inquiries, and social media engagement, setting clear success targets.

This strategic approach not only helps them focus their marketing efforts effectively, but also enables them to measure the impact of their initiatives accurately and adjust their strategies as needed for optimal results. Ultimately, this data-driven methodology positions the tourism board to enhance visibility and attract more visitors during typically slower travel periods.

2. Analyze Engagement and Conversion Data

Dive deep into the data generated from your campaign, focusing on engagement and conversion metrics. Analyze how your audience interacted with your content, which channels drove the most conversions, and what messages resonated most effectively. This analysis provides insights into audience preferences and behaviors, informing future targeting and messaging strategies.

A subscription box service analyzed its campaign data to identify which promotional offers had the highest conversion rates. They gained insights into what motivated their audience to subscribe, allowing them to improve their offers and messaging strategies. This adjustment boosted marketing effectiveness, increased engagement, and improved customer acquisition. Ultimately, this data-driven methodology allowed them to create a more compelling value proposition that resonated strongly with their target market.

3. Identify Areas for Improvement

Every campaign, regardless of its success, offers opportunities for improvement. Identify areas where your strategy could have been more effective, whether it's in targeting, messaging, or execution. Recognizing these areas helps you improve your strategy, ensuring future campaigns learn from past experiences.

A software company highlighted the need for thorough analysis by examining a recent product launch campaign that fell short of expectations. Through this review, they were able to pinpoint specific gaps in their educational content that hindered the campaign's success.

They created a plan to improve their next launch by using better resources and targeted strategies to connect more effectively with their audience. This proactive approach not only aims to rectify past mistakes but also sets a solid foundation for future initiatives.

4. Gather Qualitative Feedback

Qualitative feedback is essential for gaining deeper insights into customer perceptions and experiences and analyzing quantitative data. To gather valuable information, actively seek feedback from your audience using surveys, interviews, or social media interactions.

This feedback highlights the emotional aspects of your campaign and identifies areas for improvement to enhance the customer journey. By understanding these insights, you can better tailor your efforts to meet the needs and desires of your audience.

A boutique hotel chain demonstrated this strategy by carefully collecting and analyzing guest feedback after launching a new loyalty program. By understanding what guests liked and what they found lacking, the hotel improved its programs and communication strategies.

As a result of these adjustments, they not only enhanced customer satisfaction but also fostered deeper loyalty among their clients. This proactive approach demonstrates the importance of listening to guests in creating a more appealing and effective loyalty initiative.

5. Evaluate Competitive Positioning

Assessing the impact of your campaign on your competitive positioning in the market is crucial for understanding its effectiveness. Evaluate if your efforts have changed consumer perceptions of your brand and improved its visibility on different platforms. Furthermore, consider how these initiatives may have differentiated your offerings from competitors, making them more appealing to your target audience. This evaluation will offer insights into your market position and guide strategic decisions to strengthen it and enhance your competitive advantages.

A local coffee roaster strategically evaluated how its sustainable sourcing campaign affected consumers' perception of the brand. By analyzing competitor responses and consumer sentiment, they identified effective ways to highlight their commitment to sustainability. This improved their ability to communicate their values and strengthened their unique market position. Ultimately, these insights allowed them to better connect with their target audience and enhance their brand reputation.

6. Document Insights and Learnings

Produce a thorough and detailed report that encapsulates the insights gained and lessons learned from your recent campaign assessment. This document should outline key findings, identify areas for improvement, and offer actionable recommendations for future campaigns. Keeping track of these insights creates a valuable knowledge base that will enhance your strategic approach and decision-making in the future.

A regional healthcare provider showcased the success of its patient outreach campaign by carefully documenting its insights. By examining the strategies that most effectively engaged their audience, they developed a robust set of best practices to inform and enhance their future initiatives. This thorough evaluation not only enhanced patient engagement but also led to a remarkable improvement in overall care outcomes, highlighting the catalytic effect of informed decision-making in healthcare. Ultimately, their approach is a valuable model for other providers aiming to enhance their connection with patients.

7. Foster a Culture of Continuous Improvement

Embed a mindset of continuous improvement within your organization, encouraging team members to view every campaign as an opportunity for learning and growth. Foster open discussions about campaign outcomes, celebrating successes, and constructively addressing challenges. This culture ensures that your team remains adaptable and innovative, consistently striving for excellence.

An educational institution fully embraced this collaborative culture by actively hosting post-campaign debrief sessions involving faculty and staff members. These well-organized gatherings fostered open communication and collaboration, facilitating a valuable exchange of insights and experiences.

This resulted in a vibrant atmosphere for knowledge exchange, creating more sophisticated and impactful outreach strategies designed to engage prospective students. Ultimately, this initiative has significantly enhanced the institution's ability to connect with and engage potential learners in a meaningful way.

Conducting a thorough battle damage assessment transforms campaign analysis from a routine task into a strategic advantage. By extracting insights and learnings, you ensure that every campaign contributes to your business's evolution, refining your approach and enhancing your adaptability.

As we dive deeper into the SMAC Framework, keep in mind that adaptability extends beyond merely responding to change; it involves drawing insights from every experience and strategically evolving.

By implementing a comprehensive assessment process, you're well-equipped to tackle future campaigns with confidence, guaranteeing that your marketing initiatives stay relevant and impactful.

Prepare to leverage these insights as you advance through the SMAC Framework, turning every campaign into a stepping stone for growth and innovation. Embracing adaptability helps you navigate market complexities, ensuring your brand succeeds in a changing environment.

Common Traps

Adaptation Killers

Waiting too long to change because a strategy "used to work."

- Ignoring early warning signals from data or customer feedback.

- Letting ego override evidence.

- Overcorrecting without testing.

- Failing to document and learn from failed attempts.

Strategic Evolution Framework

As we conclude our exploration of adaptability within the SMAC Framework, it's crucial to highlight the strategic evolution framework that ensures your brand not only survives but thrives in an ever-changing marketplace. Adaptability is more than just surviving; it's evolving strategically to meet future challenges head-on. This final section ties together our insights, setting the stage for sustained growth and innovation.

"No strategy survives first contact with the enemy.
The battlefield always rewrites the plan."

Looking back on my Navy experiences, a pivotal moment comes to mind—a time when our ship had to rethink its strategies after a challenging mission. Rather than simply repeating past actions, we paused to assess, adapt, and develop a new operational framework designed to tackle unforeseen challenges more effectively.

Our capacity to evolve strategically, rather than becoming complacent, played a crucial role in turning obstacles into opportunities for growth. In marketing, strategic evolution keeps your brand strong and innovative, allowing you to seize new opportunities.

To build a robust strategic evolution framework, focus on these key elements, each tailored to make your business agile, innovative, and strategically aligned:

Develop Long-Term Vision and Goals

At the heart of every successful strategic framework lies a well-defined long-term vision. Establish a clear vision for the future of your business and create specific, measurable goals that support this vision. This long-term perspective provides direction, ensuring that short-term actions contribute to your overarching strategic objectives.

Here's a compelling example of a business that successfully implemented this approach. A regional clothing retailer set an ambitious vision to become a recognized leader in sustainable fashion within the industry. They set ambitious goals aimed at minimizing their environmental footprint while prioritizing the use of ethically sourced materials.

This initiative established a solid framework that not only guided their product development but also effectively shaped their marketing strategies. This alignment ensured that daily operations reflected their long-term mission, promoting a strong commitment to sustainability throughout the entire organization.

Embed Continuous Learning

I know I have mentioned this point previously, but it bears repeating for emphasis. Incorporating continuous learning into your strategy is crucial to keep your business adaptable and informed in a changing environment. This requires not just motivating team members to stay informed about industry trends, consumer behaviors, and technological advancements, but also cultivating a supportive environment that fosters continuous learning and personal growth.

Fostering a culture of continuous learning within your organization not only sharpens individual skills but also equips the entire team to effectively tackle the diverse challenges posed by the rapidly evolving business landscape. This proactive approach helps your organization stay flexible and ready to seize new opportunities. Ultimately, this investment in learning fosters innovation and resilience, positioning your organization for long-term success in a constantly evolving market.

A local family-owned plumbing business shows the value of investing in its workforce through ongoing training and development, understanding that skilled employees are key to success. By staying updated on the latest plumbing and home service technologies, they retained their competitive edge and created a culture of learning that helped keep key team members.

Their focus on innovation kept their products relevant to customer needs, boosting their community reputation. Through these efforts, the business demonstrated how prioritizing employee growth can lead to sustained success and customer satisfaction.

Encourage Strategic Experimentation

This is a crucial recommendation that can significantly influence the success and advancement of your business in today's competitive landscape. We should promote a culture of strategic experimentation that embraces calculated risks and values the lessons learned from failures. This innovative mindset encourages your company to explore new ideas without the fear of failure that can hinder creativity and progress. By fully committing to strategic experimentation, you will discover fresh growth opportunities and enhance your business's ability to distinguish itself from the competition, paving the way for long-term success.

A small craft brewery embraced innovation by experimenting with limited-edition seasonal beers. These creative trials offered insights into consumer preferences and helped brewers perfect their flavors. By meticulously evaluating their audience's preferences throughout this process, they successfully launched a new flagship product that truly resonated with consumers. This flagship offering became a beloved choice for their customers, solidifying the brewery's reputation in the competitive craft beer market.

Align Resources with Strategic Priorities

This is truly invaluable advice that I wish I had been aware of much earlier in my career journey. It is essential to guarantee that all your resources—financial, human, and technological—are readily available and strategically aligned with your core priorities. To make sure this happens, it's key to consistently evaluate and analyze your resource allocation, verifying that it effectively aligns with and supports your long-term objectives and growth initiatives. This alignment ensures that your efforts are precisely focused and highly efficient, maximizing both your impact and overall effectiveness in all your endeavors.

A fast-growing medical family practice is showing its commitment to innovation and quality care by boosting its telehealth initiatives. They focused on advanced digital technology and thorough staff training, leading to a great improvement in healthcare access for patients. This focus improved the patient experience and increased satisfaction, aligning services with the changing needs of the healthcare industry. Their proactive approach established the practice as a community leader, demonstrating their commitment to modern solutions and high-quality care.

Implement Agile Decision-Making Processes

Embracing agile decision-making processes is crucial for any business striving to remain competitive in today's rapidly evolving landscape. This approach enables swift adaptations to market fluctuations and the seizing of emerging opportunities. Organizations can promote cross-functional collaboration to empower teams to make quick, informed decisions using real-time data and insights. This agility improves responsiveness and helps the organization be proactive, resulting in greater resilience and success in a changing market.

An e-commerce platform effectively harnessed the potential of agile project management methodologies to significantly enhance its operations. By emphasizing swift decision-making and cultivating a collaborative environment among teams, the platform significantly accelerated its product development cycles. This approach enabled them to respond faster to consumer feedback and enhanced their adaptability to changing market trends. Ultimately, these practices positioned the platform for greater success in a competitive landscape where responsiveness is key.

Build Strategic Partnerships

Strategic partnerships can extend your capabilities and amplify your reach. Identify partners who align with your values and strategic objectives, and collaborate to create mutually beneficial opportunities. These partnerships can enhance your offerings, access new markets, and drive innovation.

A local coffee shop showcased the benefits of collaboration by teaming up with a nearby bakery, enhancing the experience for its customers. This partnership enabled both businesses to offer unique coffee and pastry pairings, attracting a wider audience eager to try them.

Both establishments saw improved brand loyalty as customers connected their brands with quality products and enjoyable experiences. This strategic alliance demonstrates how collaboration fosters growth and customer engagement for small businesses in the community.

Measure Progress and Adapt

Consistently assess your progress in relation to your strategic goals and be flexible in adapting your framework as circumstances evolve. Leverage key performance indicators (KPIs) to monitor your success and pinpoint specific areas ripe for enhancement.

Refining your framework is crucial for ensuring that your business remains aligned with its overarching vision. It also equips your organization to effectively tackle any future challenges that may arise.

A solar energy installation company demonstrated its dedication to customer satisfaction by performing comprehensive annual strategic reviews. The assessments evaluated how well customers met their renewable energy goals and adjusted strategies based on changing market conditions. This detailed analysis revealed a rising customer demand for in-home powerwalls, significantly amplifying the benefits of solar panel systems. This valuable insight not only enabled them to enhance their offerings but also secured their trajectory toward sustaining their leadership position within the industry.

The strategic evolution framework is your roadmap for achieving long-term success in an ever-changing market. Integrating adaptability into your strategy helps your business thrive in uncertainty, turning challenges into opportunities for innovation and growth.

Strategic evolution isn't a one-time plan—it's a loop of learning, testing, adjusting, and scaling. Your business must evolve like software: frequent updates, not a once-a-year overhaul.

As we wrap up this chapter on adaptability, it's vital to understand that evolution involves more than just responding to change; it's about taking the initiative to shape the future of your business. A well-defined strategic framework empowers you to navigate the market with confidence, ensuring your brand remains relevant and influential.

Harness these insights as you progress through the SMAC Framework, transforming adaptability into a fundamental element of your strategic execution. Armed with a clear vision and a relentless dedication to continuous improvement, you adeptly maneuver through the ever-evolving market landscape, ensuring your brand not only survives but thrives amidst the challenges of change.

The businesses that dominate tomorrow aren't the ones with the best current plan. They're the ones that adapt today. Stay flexible. Stay curious. Stay lethal.

Real-World Case Study: Warby Parker— Adaptability to Revolutionize Eyewear

In 2010, the eyewear industry was primarily ruled by one dominant player: Luxottica. This powerhouse controlled a significant portion of the market through its renowned brands, such as Ray-Ban, Oakley, and Persol, and owned key retail outlets like LensCrafters and Sunglass Hut. This monopoly resulted in skyrocketing prices for consumers, leaving them with no option but to spend hundreds of dollars on prescription glasses.

Enter Warby Parker, a disruptive start-up founded by four Wharton MBA students who believed buying stylish, high-quality eyewear shouldn't cost a fortune. With a groundbreaking business model and unparalleled flexibility, Warby Parker revolutionized the eyewear industry, transforming how consumers shop for glasses.

Intelligence-Gathering Systems

Warby Parker's founders began with an incisive understanding of the problem: prescription eyewear was overpriced and inconvenient to purchase. Consumers often had to visit physical stores, pay steep prices, and wait weeks for their glasses to be ready. Warby Parker saw a chance to sell stylish, high-quality glasses directly to consumers (DTC), cutting out middlemen and reducing costs.

But their adaptability didn't stop there. The company relied heavily on consumer feedback to refine its offerings. They implemented robust data collection systems to track customer preferences, from frame styles to the ideal user experience. This intelligence gathering allowed Warby Parker to stay agile and continuously optimize its products and services.

Battle Damage Assessment (Analytics & Optimization)

Warby Parker didn't just disrupt an industry—they rewrote the rules. Their first big test? Convincing people to buy glasses without ever trying them on. Eyewear is a highly personal purchase, and many consumers were hesitant to order frames without trying them on first. Warby Parker brilliantly seized the opportunity to enhance customer experience by launching their Home Try-On Program, enabling customers to confidently order up to five pairs of glasses to try at home for free.

The program proved to be an instant success, showcasing Warby Parker's skill in adapting to customer needs and effectively addressing a significant challenge in their business model. The company tracked conversion rates and customer feedback to fine-tune the program, ensuring it maximized both user satisfaction and profitability.

Strategic Evolution Framework

As Warby Parker expanded, they refused to become complacent. Instead, they innovatively combined e-commerce with brick-and-mortar stores, creating a dynamic business model. As traditional retailers struggled to adapt to the surge of online shopping, Warby Parker effortlessly embraced an omnichannel strategy, establishing itself as a leader in the industry.

They strategically launched brick-and-mortar stores in prime locations, allowing customers to try on glasses in person while enjoying the cost advantages of their direct-to-consumer model. These stores weren't just transactional—they were designed to be experiential, reinforcing the brand's modern, customer-centric ethos.

Pivoting to Serve Emerging Trends

Recognizing that many customers lacked current prescriptions, Warby Parker innovatively responded by offering in-store eye exams and launching a virtual vision test app. This move addressed a significant barrier to purchase and further cemented Warby Parker's position as a customer-focused innovator.

Additionally, as sustainability became a priority for consumers, Warby Parker responded by emphasizing its commitment to environmental responsibility. Their "Buy a Pair, Give a Pair" initiative donates glasses to those in need, reflecting the brand's commitment to social responsibility and fostering stronger customer loyalty.

The Outcome: Disruptor Turned Household Name

Warby Parker has evolved from a niche disruptor into one of the most well-known brands in eyewear, currently valued at over $3 billion. Their ability to adapt to customer needs and use data to refine their approach has helped them thrive in an industry previously dominated by a monopoly.

Warby Parker's story demonstrates the power of adaptability, as highlighted in Chapter 5. Through relentless intelligence gathering, performance evaluation, and strategic evolution, it not only competed with Luxottica but also revolutionized the eyewear industry.

Warby Parker didn't just react to disruption—they redefined the category by listening, testing, and evolving with customer behavior. Adaptation wasn't their fallback—it was their offensive strategy.

Chapter 5 Key Takeaways: ADAPT—The Art of Strategic Evolution

"In war, the plan is nothing, but planning is everything."
—Dwight D. Eisenhower

KEY LEARNING POINTS

◆ **Adapt or Die: The Harsh Reality of Business Warfare**

Marketing is **never static**—consumer behavior shifts, technology evolves, and competitors won't stay in their lanes. The businesses that refuse to adapt? **They get crushed.**

Winning in the digital battlefield means **embracing change, evolving strategies, and making adjustments before the market forces you to.**

◆ **The Myth of the Perfect Strategy**

Too many businesses waste time trying to create the **"perfect" marketing plan**—only to watch it fail when reality doesn't match expectations.

- **The battlefield changes.** No strategy survives first contact with the enemy.

- **Data reveals the truth.** Your audience will tell you what works—if you listen.

- **Small adjustments create massive results.** Micro-pivots based on real-time feedback lead to continuous improvement.

- **Ego is the enemy.** Clinging to a failing strategy because it's "your idea" will kill your business.

◆ The OODA Loop: Adapt Like a Fighter Pilot

Military strategist John Boyd created the **OODA Loop**—a process elite fighter pilots use to outmaneuver their enemies in split seconds.

✓ Observe: Gather intelligence—what's happening in your market?

✓ Orient: Analyze the data and understand what it means for your business.

✓ Decide: Choose the best course of action based on what you know.

✓ Act: Execute quickly—before your competitors do.

Repeat the cycle continuously to stay ahead.

◆ Agility is the Competitive Advantage of Underdogs

"Big corporations take months to adapt. Their approval processes, outdated hierarchies, and internal politics slow them down. Your advantage? Speed and flexibility."

✅ You can change messaging in real time.

✅ You can pivot offers based on customer demand.

✅ You can test and tweak campaigns while competitors are still "reviewing data."

◆ The War is Won by the Businesses That Pivot Before the Market Demands It

✗ Businesses that wait too long to change get **wiped out**.

✅ Businesses that pivot **proactively** dominate the market.

◆ How to Build an Adaptive Marketing Strategy

⊘ **Measure what matters.** Are you tracking vanity metrics or real performance indicators?

⊘ **Develop "kill switches."** If a campaign isn't working, **cut it fast.** No hesitation.

⊘ **Run small experiments.** Test **before** making big bets.

⊘ **Stay paranoid.** Never assume your strategy is "good enough." Always look for the next move.

Action Steps to Master Adaptability

⊘ Identify **one failing marketing effort** and either improve or eliminate it.

⊘ Review your data weekly—what insights should drive your next move?

⊘ Set up **a rapid testing system** to refine your messaging, offers, and targeting.

⊘ Schedule a **quarterly strategy review** to stay ahead of industry shifts.

⊘ Ask yourself daily: **"What do I need to change today to stay ahead?"**

Final thought: *"The businesses that dominate aren't the ones with the best original plan. They're the ones that adapt before they have to. Stay flexible. Stay fast. Stay lethal."*

CHAPTER 6

COMMUNICATE—Command & Control

"The single biggest problem in communication
is the illusion that it has taken place."
—George Bernard Shaw

Mission Brief: CHAPTER 6 – COMMUNICATE: Command & Control

On the battlefield, poor communication costs lives. In business, it costs attention, trust, and customers. When your message isn't clear, someone else will fill the silence—and it won't be in your favor.

Your mission:

Establish control through clarity. Rally your audience with a message that cuts through the noise and aligns every channel to your cause. This chapter gives you the tools to speak with authority, consistency, and precision—because when you control the message, you control the market.

The next key element of the SMAC Framework is communication, an essential factor that connects your strategic efforts.

"In the crowded field of digital marketing, clear communication is essential for making an impact."

This chapter focuses on mastering communication to ensure your message resonates effectively with your audience.

During my time as a young sailor in the U.S. Navy, one mission stands out where communication made—or could have broken—the entire operation. Our mission required skillfully coordinating a sophisticated multi-ship maneuver through the treacherous waters of the Straits of Hormuz, situated off the coast of Iran, during the turbulent conflict between Iran and Iraq.

In such a high-stakes environment, where effective communication was crucial, even the slightest misstep could spell disaster. Through clear, concise, and timely communication, we navigated the challenge seamlessly, achieving our objectives precisely.

That mission taught me this: in any mission—military or marketing—communication is the real force multiplier. It fosters alignment, builds trust, and ensures everyone moves in concert toward a common goal.

In marketing, communication is the thread that weaves your strategy into a cohesive narrative. It's not just about sending messages—it's about creating meaningful interactions that connect with your audience and strengthen your brand. This chapter will teach you the key aspects of communication, helping you engage effectively.

> *"It's not just what you say—it's how consistently, clearly, and compellingly you say it."* –Kevin McGrew

The 3 Laws of Combat-Ready Messaging

- **Clear** – If they don't get it in 5 seconds, you've lost.

- **Concise** – Say more with less. Every word is ammo.

- **Compelling** – If it doesn't move them, it's just noise.

We'll explore the importance of message clarity, which lays the foundation for impactful communication. *A clear and compelling message cuts through the clutter, capturing attention and driving action.* By honing your message, you ensure it resonates with your audience, aligning with their needs and aspirations.

A supplement company stood out in a competitive market by simplifying its product range into a clear value proposition that addressed customer challenges. This clarity improved brand recognition and fostered stronger connections with customers, enhancing loyalty and trust. By clearly communicating value, they broke through the noise—and gave overwhelmed customers a reason to care.

We'll also explore the concept of cross-channel communication, a powerful strategy that ensures your message connects—wherever your audience is. Integrating your communication efforts across multiple platforms creates a cohesive brand experience that amplifies your message and deepens your connection with your audience.

In this chapter, we will explore the incredible impact of cultivating an army of advocates—dedicated customers who endorse your brand, amplify your message, and significantly expand your reach. By engaging authentically and building relationships, **you turn customers into brand advocates who buy, promote, and defend your brand.**

Communication isn't broadcasting. It's connecting. The brands that win speak with their audience—not at them. Every word and interaction counts in making your message meaningful and memorable.

Get ready to engage with intention and precision as we delve into this chapter, transforming communication into a fundamental element of your strategic execution. By prioritizing effective communication, you elevate your brand's voice above the clutter, delivering messages that resonate powerfully with your most important audience.

Welcome to the front lines of modern marketing—where storytelling and strategy collide. This chapter will arm you with the tools to speak with clarity, lead with consistency, and build a message strong enough to command attention. As we continue through the SMAC Framework, let these insights guide your journey toward marketing mastery and lasting brand impact.

Message Clarity and Force Multiplication

In the vibrant marketplace of ideas, where messages vie for attention, the clarity of your communication can determine whether you are heard or overlooked. Effective marketing hinges on clear communication, which guarantees that your message not only reaches your audience but also resonates with them. In this section, we'll dive into the art of crafting a message that cuts through the noise, capturing attention and driving meaningful engagement.

During my time in the Navy, I encountered a mission that underscored the critical importance of clear communication. We undertook the task of orchestrating a complex operation involving multiple vessels within a multinational task force, where it was paramount that every directive was communicated with complete clarity and precision, leaving no room for misunderstanding. We had to eliminate jargon and extraneous details, honing in on the vital information necessary for everyone to grasp.

This experience highlighted that clarity goes beyond mere simplicity; it embodies precision in conveying messages effectively. In marketing, this translates into crafting messages that speak directly to your audience's needs and desires without clutter or confusion.

To achieve message clarity, focus on refining your core message to match your audience's expectations. Here are ways to ensure your communication is clear and impactful:

Understand Your Audience

To create a message that is both clear and impactful, it is crucial to thoroughly understand your audience, identifying not just who they are, but also what they truly value. This means diving deep into their needs, preferences, and the challenges they face in their daily lives.

By understanding their experiences and viewing things from their perspective, you can customize your message to perfectly align with their expectations. This thoughtful alignment will guarantee that your communication directly addresses their unique challenges and aspirations, making it far more impactful and engaging.

A wealth management firm targeting young professionals is crafting messages that highlight financial independence and effective wealth-building strategies. By highlighting these themes, the firm guarantees that its messaging not only engages this demographic but also resonates deeply with their aspirations and fundamental values.

Furthermore, the firm aims to instill a powerful sense of empowerment and ambition, motivating young professionals to seize control of their financial destinies while fully engaging with the services provided. This personalized approach is essential for building strong, lasting relationships with clients who want to grow their wealth and achieve financial independence.

Define Your Core Message

Your core message is the essence of what you want to communicate. It should be concise, compelling, and aligned with your brand's value proposition. Focus on the key benefits and unique selling points that differentiate your offering from competitors. By distilling your message to its core, you ensure it is memorable and impactful.

A medical device start-up successfully refined its messaging strategy by highlighting the unique features of its groundbreaking product, which dramatically elevates the sleep experience and enhances overall sleep quality.

This clear communication appealed to young adults dealing with sleep issues and seeking noninvasive solutions. The targeted messaging effectively captivated the intended audience, significantly boosting brand awareness and enhancing engagement levels among potential customers. The start-up strategically addressed a relatable pain point, successfully establishing itself as an attractive choice in the wellness market.

Use Clear and Concise Language

Avoid jargon and overly complex language that can obscure your message. Use straightforward language that is easy to understand and relatable to your audience. This approach not only enhances comprehension but also builds trust, as it demonstrates your commitment to transparent and honest communication.

A pulmonary care provider improved patient communication by simplifying complex medical information, making it more accessible and understandable. Using clear language to explain medical procedures, conditions, and treatments improved patient understanding and satisfaction.

This insightful strategy not only enhanced comprehension but also significantly strengthened relationships with patients, fostering enduring trust between them and the healthcare team. In turn, these improved interactions fostered a more positive healthcare experience for everyone involved.

Align Visuals with Your Message

Visual elements play a critical role in reinforcing your message. Ensure that your visuals align with your core message and enhance its clarity. Incorporate visuals like imagery, infographics, and design elements to enhance your narrative and help your audience understand and remember your message more effectively.

An adventure travel agency masterfully highlighted its offerings through vibrant and inspirational visuals, capturing the spirit of the exhilarating experiences it delivers. The visuals appealed to the adventurous spirit in the agency's messaging, effectively attracting potential travelers. This effective use of visual communication attracted more interest and significantly boosted inquiries and bookings from enthusiastic adventurers ready to explore.

Test and Refine Your Message

Effective communication is an iterative process. Test your message with a sample audience to gauge its clarity and impact. Solicit feedback and use it to refine your message, ensuring it resonates as intended. This process of testing and refinement ensures that your communication remains relevant and effective.

Food for the Hungry, a nonprofit organization, adopted this approach by conducting focus groups to test its fundraising appeals. They found that their email messaging, which focused on facts and statistics, was not as effective as their story-based direct mail campaigns. By using participant feedback, they improved their messaging to showcase the impact of donations through consistent storytelling, focusing on beneficiary narratives instead of just informational content. This strategic shift increased engagement and improved fundraising performance across their communication platforms.

Maintain Consistency Across Channels

Consistency is key to reinforcing your message across multiple channels. Ensure your core message remains consistent, whether communicated through social media, email, or traditional advertising. This consistency builds brand recognition and reinforces your message, making it more likely to resonate with your audience.

Poppy Handcrafted Popcorn effectively showcases its dedication to quality by ensuring that its messaging remains consistent across every customer touchpoint. With each interaction, from their strikingly vibrant packaging to their dynamic and engaging social media presence, they consistently showcase their dedication to providing premium, artisanal snacks. This careful focus on maintaining brand consistency not only reinforces their brand identity but also significantly contributes to the development and strengthening of customer loyalty over time.

Leverage Emotional Appeal

Emotions are powerful drivers of engagement and action. Infuse your message with emotional appeal, connecting with your audience on a deeper, more personal level. Whether tapping into feelings of aspiration, nostalgia, or urgency, leveraging emotion can amplify the impact of your message.

Princess Polly, a boutique clothing retailer, successfully used emotional appeal to promote individuality and confidence in their messages. Their marketing communications use relatable, youth-focused language like "hella cute" and "babe" while encouraging customers to express their unique style through user-generated content.

They connected emotionally with customers by appealing to their desire for self-expression, resulting in strong brand loyalty and repeat purchases, with up to 73x ROI on personalized SMS campaigns. Their success is clear from the numerous "Princess Polly haul" videos and active social media engagement on platforms like Instagram, TikTok, and Snapchat, where customers share their personal style stories.

The art of clear communication is about making your message not only heard but felt. By gaining insights into your audience and tailoring a message that resonates with them, you foster powerful connections that enhance engagement and cultivate loyalty. This clarity ensures that your brand's voice rises above the noise, resonating with those who matter most.

As we continue exploring the SMAC Framework, remember that effective communication is a cornerstone of strategic execution. By delivering a clear and compelling message, you establish the groundwork for meaningful engagement, ensuring that your brand's narrative is communicated with both precision and strength.

Harness these insights as you navigate the SMAC Framework, transforming effective communication into a formidable force for enhancing your brand's impact. By focusing on clarity, you confidently navigate market complexities, making your brand stand out and appealing to your audience.

"In battle, the right communication can turn a platoon into an army. In marketing, a sharp message multiplies your impact across every channel." –Kevin McGrew

Cross-Channel Communication Strategy

As we deepen our exploration of communication within the SMAC Framework, we turn to the intricate dance of cross-channel communication. In a world where consumers interact with brands across a multitude of platforms, the ability to maintain a cohesive and consistent message is paramount. This section explores strategies to maintain a consistent and impactful message across all delivery channels.

As I reflect on my past experiences, one naval operation stands out for its emphasis on coordination. Our mission involved managing communications among several vessels during underway replenishment operations, each facing unique responsibilities and challenges.

The mission's success depended on our ability to maintain a smooth flow of information, making our role essential to the operation. In marketing, cross-channel communication plays a crucial role by uniting your strategic initiatives into a cohesive framework that effectively captures and maintains audience engagement.

Cross-channel communication involves more than just being on different platforms; it's about creating a consistent brand experience that enhances your message and strengthens relationships with your audience. Here's how you can master cross-channel communication to enhance your brand's impact and reach:

Establish a Unified Brand Voice

A consistent brand voice is crucial for clear communication across different channels. Defining your brand's tone, style, and detailed messaging guidelines is essential. These elements should not only reflect your overall value proposition but also create a strong connection with your target audience.

By fostering this consistency, you enhance strong brand recognition and build trust with your consumers, ultimately solidifying your core message across all customer interactions. The outcome is a cohesive experience that enhances customer loyalty and engagement with your brand.

MoonPie, a century-old marshmallow sandwich brand, maintains a fun and friendly tone in all its communications, which boosts customer engagement. The brand's quirky and self-deprecating tone in social media, newsletters, and customer service creates a cohesive experience, turning a simple snack into a beloved cultural icon.

Since 1917, when a Kentucky coal miner asked for a snack "as big as the moon," MoonPie has transformed from a working-class treat into a popular lifestyle brand, producing one million pies daily.

Their unique social media presence reflects their heritage and builds customer loyalty, particularly among younger audiences. This strategy has helped MoonPie cultivate a vibrant community around their brand, where customers feel connected to the product's nostalgia and contemporary relevance, leading to record sales and recognition as Social Media Brand of the Year by *Forbes Magazine* in 2018.

Identify Key Channels for Engagement

Not all channels are relevant for every brand. Identify the platforms where your audience is most active and engaged, focusing your efforts on these key touchpoints. By prioritizing the channels that align with your audience's preferences, you ensure your message is delivered effectively and efficiently.

The Squad, a fitness chain from Cork, Ireland, has successfully focused its marketing on Instagram and engaged in local community events. Through visually appealing content and the #ImWithTheSquad campaign, they engaged fitness enthusiasts and strengthened their community presence.

Their strategy of engaging online and fostering meaningful in-person interactions has successfully attracted over 60 participants per session and expanded their online global attendance and reach to places like America, Abu Dhabi, and London.

Through their commitment to creating an authentic community, owners Kate and Josie have elevated The Squad beyond a mere fitness center; they have nurtured a vibrant network of wellness enthusiasts. Their dedication to building relationships has positioned The Squad as a reliable destination for health and fitness in the area. Their focus on balancing promotional content with real community engagement has earned them nearly 8,000 active members participating in both online and in-person fitness activities.

Tailor Content for Each Platform

Consistent messaging is essential for brand recognition and trust, but it's also important to customize content for each platform's unique features. This requires choosing the right format for each platform, understanding the audience's expectations, and adhering to best practices for engagement.

Adapting your content can greatly improve its relevance and impact, helping you connect better with your audience. This balance between consistency and adaptability is key to effective communication in today's diverse digital landscape.

HubSpot masterfully demonstrates this idea by skillfully customizing its content strategy for different platforms. They effectively communicated their main message about inbound marketing and business growth using impactful visuals and brief statistics designed for social media. They created in-depth articles on complex marketing ideas for their blog and produced engaging videos for YouTube. Each piece of content was meticulously optimized to connect with its specific audience, channel, and audience preferences.

This comprehensive strategy not only expanded their reach and positioned them as thought leaders in the industry, but it also significantly boosted user engagement and lead generation across all platforms.

Integrate Communication Efforts

Integration is key to ensuring your cross-channel communication remains cohesive. Develop integrated campaigns that span multiple platforms, reinforcing your message and maximizing reach. By coordinating your efforts, you create a seamless brand experience that resonates with your audience.

Montirex, a rapidly growing sportswear brand, effectively utilizes integrated marketing through innovative campaigns. By unifying email and SMS marketing with Klaviyo, they create a cohesive multi-channel strategy targeting their young audience. Their abandoned cart flow reengages shoppers with tailored discounts via email and SMS, generating 30% of Klaviyo-attributed revenue. Exclusive SMS deals foster a sense of community with a 9.3% average click rate.

Additionally, their "Break the Wall" campaign addresses mental health stigma through various advertising and events, enhancing engagement and brand identity. Overall, Montirex's coordinated efforts boost sales and foster long-term loyalty.

Leverage Data and Insights

Utilizing data and insights is essential for informing and enhancing your cross-channel communication strategy. By conducting a comprehensive analysis of audience behavior and preferences across different platforms, you can enhance your messaging to more effectively connect with your target audience, leading to a substantial boost in engagement levels.

Utilizing this invaluable data allows you to customize your communication effectively, ensuring it is contextual, relevant, and powerful enough to capture your audience's attention. Ultimately, this strategic approach aids in fostering stronger connections and long-lasting relationships with your customers.

Together Credit Union successfully leveraged customer interaction data to pinpoint the most effective communication channels. With $2 billion in assets and 30 branches, they improved from a two-month reporting delay to real-time analytics, showcasing member engagement preferences.

Emphasizing platforms that foster high customer interaction has significantly enhanced the overall experience. Branch managers accessed metrics and insights instantly, allowing for informed decisions on service and engagement strategies.

This targeted approach strengthened member relationships and improved retention rates, benefiting the organization. Their self-service analytics platform protected member data while offering personalized service, helping them compete with larger institutions.

Together Credit Union's data-driven strategy shows that knowing customer preferences improves outcomes for mid-sized financial institutions in competitive markets.

Monitor and Adapt to Feedback

Feedback is crucial for improving your cross-channel communication strategy and connecting better with your audience. Monitoring audience responses and engagement across platforms provides valuable insights to improve your approach.

This ongoing process is essential for ensuring your communication aligns with audience expectations and can adapt to changing market conditions. Ultimately, embracing feedback ensures that your strategy is not only effective but also relevant in an ever-evolving landscape.

The Humane Society of the United States (HSUS) effectively connected with supporters using social media and email, prioritizing interaction over just sending messages. They solicited feedback via Facebook, responded to community concerns, and tailored content to different donor capacities with custom donation options.

This approach strengthened connections with donors and volunteers, leading to nearly 5% of their funding (around $200,000) coming from Facebook. HSUS's success illustrates that meaningful dialogue fosters a dedicated network of supporters who feel connected to the mission.

Foster a Seamless Customer Journey

It is essential to ensure that your cross-channel communication strategies effectively contribute to a seamless and engaging customer journey. Identify all potential customer touchpoints with your brand to understand how customers interact with your services or products. Every interaction should build on the last to create a clear narrative that leads customers to their desired actions and outcomes. By fostering these meaningful connections, you can significantly enhance customer satisfaction and loyalty.

FTLO Travel (For the Love of Travel) has changed how millennials book group travel with its digital platform, providing a smooth experience on mobile, apps, and with concierge support. The travel profile system connected users like Sarah, 28, with like-minded travelers, creating an immediate sense of community.

This strategy boosted booking rates by 40% among 25- to 39-year-olds and achieved a 90% repeat booking rate. FTLO Travel's focus on climate neutrality and local economies attracts environmentally conscious travelers, demonstrating how a unified strategy can modernize group travel.

Cross-channel communication involves harmonizing interactions to resonate with your audience, strengthen your brand message, and foster lasting connections. Mastering cross-channel communication ensures your message is heard and felt, creating a unified and engaging brand experience.

As we continue exploring the SMAC Framework, remember that effective communication is the thread that ties your strategic efforts together. Committing to cross-channel communication establishes a strong foundation for effective engagement, keeping your brand's voice consistent and compelling.

Utilize these insights to effectively enhance cross-channel communication and boost your brand impact within the SMAC Framework. You confidently navigate the market, ensuring your brand connects consistently across all platforms.

Building Your Army of Advocates

As we conclude our exploration of communication within the SMAC Framework, we emphasize the importance of building your army of advocates through effective communication. In today's digital age, having loyal advocates who promote your brand is essential for success. This section dives into how you can transform satisfied customers into passionate advocates, amplifying your reach and influence.

A key lesson from my experiences is that our success in an operation depended on the teamwork of partner forces. The operation succeeded not just because of our skills, but also due to the support of our allies, who shared our goals. This collaboration taught me that having advocates— those who support and amplify your efforts—is a strategic advantage.

In marketing, advocates are customers who support your brand and share their experiences, helping to expand your influence beyond traditional methods.

Your Advocates Are Force Multipliers

You don't need millions of customers—you need missionaries.

- They tell your story for you.

- They defend your brand in battle.

- They extend your reach without spending a dime.

Building an army of advocates involves nurturing relationships and fostering trust, turning satisfied customers into enthusiastic promoters.

Here's how you can cultivate and empower your advocates to amplify your brand:

Deliver Exceptional Experiences

At the core of effective advocacy lies the crucial element of customer satisfaction. Deliver exceptional experiences that exceed expectations, creating memorable interactions that leave a lasting impression. Whether through superior product quality, outstanding customer service, or personalized interactions, ensure that every touchpoint enhances customer satisfaction.

Rosewood Hotels & Resorts, for instance, prioritizes personalized guest experiences by anticipating preferences and incorporating thoughtful details. This approach not only fosters loyalty but also encourages enthusiastic referrals among guests.

Their "relationship hospitality" philosophy, emphasizing genuine connections, distinguishes them in the luxury market and drives word-of-mouth marketing. Key success elements involve personalized attention through subtle gestures, authentic local experiences, and a relationship-focused approach instead of traditional loyalty programs, fostering natural brand advocates.

Foster Genuine Connections

Building authentic and meaningful relationships with your customers is essential for fostering a thriving culture of advocacy. Engage with your audience personally by showing genuine interest in their feedback and experiences.

When customers recognize that you genuinely appreciate their feedback and care about their viewpoints, it fosters a profound sense of connection and loyalty. This loyalty transforms customers into enthusiastic advocates for your brand, fostering heightened trust and paving the way for long-term success.

LEGO has brilliantly showcased its dedication to creativity and community involvement through a diverse range of initiatives designed for both children and adults. They offer creative building challenges and community events while fostering an inclusive platform that encourages personal expression and sharing for builders of all ages.

With its #RebuildTheWorld initiative, LEGO has cultivated a dynamic community of enthusiastic creators who wholeheartedly promote a culture of imagination and connection. This dedicated group eagerly shares their unique builds, inspiring one another and enriching the vast global LEGO ecosystem.

Their commitment to celebrating individual creativity and storytelling creates an empowering environment, making builders feel valued and strengthening the connection between LEGO and its diverse community.

Encourage User-Generated Content

User-generated content (UGC) is an immensely powerful asset for enhancing advocacy, increasing brand visibility, and nurturing community engagement in today's competitive market. By actively inviting your customers to share their personal experiences and stories through platforms like online reviews, heartfelt testimonials, and engaging social media posts, you foster a dynamic and vibrant community of passionate advocates who truly care.

Highlighting user-generated content not only brings an irresistible authenticity and relatability to your brand but also offers a powerful platform for dedicated supporters to fervently share their loyalty and gratitude. This approach strengthens your connection with your audience and helps build a loyal customer base that aligns with your brand message.

Aerie's #AerieREAL campaign stands as a testament to the power of user-generated content (UGC) in marketing. Aerie encouraged customers to share unretouched photos of their clothing, creating a sense of community and inclusivity. The UGC campaign boosted Aerie's body positivity message and provided genuine content for its marketing. The #AerieREAL campaign's success demonstrates how brands can leverage UGC to build trust, strengthen relationships with customers, and drive growth.

Provide Incentives for Advocacy

Incentivizing advocacy can effectively motivate customers to take an active role in promoting your brand to their friends and family. Consider the implementation of referral programs, loyalty rewards, or exclusive offers that not only acknowledge but also incentivize advocates for their passionate efforts in promoting your brand.

Offering these incentives not only fosters advocacy but also enhances the overall relationship and loyalty customers have toward your brand. In the long run, these strategies can create a thriving community of brand advocates invested in your success.

BioTrust stands out as a prime example of a brand that successfully harnesses the power of advocacy. Their meticulously structured referral program rewards existing customers while enticing new ones by offering a $20 coupon for referrers, in addition to exclusive discounts designed specifically for newcomers.

This initiative has built a strong community with over 1 million subscribers and a 33% increase in email engagement. The program strengthens community connections through a VIP Facebook Group, health challenges, and direct access to experts. BioTrust has success-fully turned many health-conscious consumers into loyal advocates by fostering genuine connections and partnering with socially responsible organizations, boosting customer retention, and thriving in the compet-itive supplement market.

Highlight Advocate Stories

Highlighting inspiring stories and remarkable achievements of your advocates is a powerful strategy to strengthen and enhance your advocacy initiatives. Sharing heartfelt testimonials, insightful case studies, and inspiring success stories allows you to vividly showcase the significant positive impact your brand has made on the lives of your customers.

Recognizing and celebrating your advocates not only honors their experi-ences but also inspires and motivates others to step forward and play a vital role in your brand's ongoing journey. Ultimately, this collective story-telling fosters a deeper connection and loyalty among your audience.

Nice Shirt. Thanks! has skillfully leveraged advocate stories to drive its success. By turning customer ideas into wearable art, they've empowered their customers to become brand advocates on social media platforms, particularly TikTok. The #niceshirtthanks hashtag showcases genuine customer reactions and unboxing experiences, creating a community that amplifies the brand's message.

This strategy has not only generated excitement and anticipation for new designs but also reinforced the brand's unique selling proposition. The success of their viral video and quick sellouts shows how effective advocate stories can be in boosting brand growth and credibility.

Engage in Two-Way Dialogue

Advocacy thrives in an environment where open communication is not just encouraged but actively practiced at all levels. Engaging in meaningful two-way dialogue with your advocates is crucial; it involves seeking their feedback and carefully considering and responding to their concerns and suggestions.

Engaging in continuous dialogue and showing authentic appreciation for their insights cultivates trust and collaboration. This approach not only strengthens relationships but also underscores your dedication to ongoing improvement and positive evolution. This proactive approach strengthens relationships and enhances the overall effectiveness of your advocacy efforts.

TechSoup is a global nonprofit that connects the technology sector with nonprofits, transforming how these organizations use technology to fulfill their missions. Through its online community platform, TechSoup has enabled seamless communication and information sharing between volunteers and employees.

This success can be attributed to its emphasis on clear communication, consistent engagement, and a robust recognition system for contributors. The platform has improved traditional volunteer interactions, strengthened relationships, and helped quickly identify and solve challenges. TechSoup's inclusive approach combines volunteers and staff, creating a collaborative environment that serves as a model for other nonprofits and organizations.

Measure and Celebrate Advocacy

Track and measure advocacy efforts to understand their impact on your brand. Use metrics such as Net Promoter Score (NPS), referral rates, and social media mentions to assess advocacy levels. Celebrate these achievements internally and externally, recognizing advocates who go above and beyond in supporting your brand.

Civista Bank's Social Star Program showcases effective advocate appreciation within an organization. Civista honors individual employees through quarterly recognition events and lively digital celebrations, helping them build personal brands and showcase their contributions to the business.

This strategy promotes ongoing engagement and showcases the benefits of advocacy, building a strong community of loyal supporters who amplify the bank's message and influence. These initiatives boost employee motivation and improve Civista Bank's brand reputation, strengthening its industry position.

In wrapping up this chapter on communication, remember that advocacy showcases the powerful impact of effective communication. By cultivating a network of advocates who passionately support your brand, you guarantee that your message not only reaches a wider audience but also creates a lasting impression, fostering enduring impact and success.

Use these insights to enhance the SMAC Framework and make advocacy a strong force for brand impact. By cultivating authentic relationships and empowering advocates, you skillfully navigate the intricate market landscape with assurance, allowing your brand to flourish amidst the chaos and truly resonate with your audience.

Real-World Case Study: Liquid Death— Commanding the Message to Crush the Competition

The bottled water market is among the most saturated in the world, heavily controlled by industry giants such as Coca-Cola with its Dasani brand and PepsiCo's Aquafina. These brands relied on polished advertising and broad appeal to sell what was, at its core, a simple commodity: water.

In 2019, Liquid Death—a canned water start-up—entered this crowded battlefield with a radically different approach. With bold humor and a strong mission, Liquid Death captured attention, challenged stereotypes, and built a dedicated community.

Message Clarity and Force Multiplication

Liquid Death's founder, Mike Cessario, understood one thing very clearly: its water wasn't just water—it was rebellion in a can. Their message was simple yet audacious: "Murder your thirst." With slogans like this, they reframed water as a lifestyle product that appealed to a counterculture audience tired of corporate messaging.

Unlike traditional water brands, Liquid Death leaned into an edgy, irreverent tone, using skull imagery and metal-inspired branding. This wasn't just about hydration—it was about attitude. Their clarity of purpose and ability to resonate with their audience turned a mundane product into a conversation starter.

Cross-Channel Communication Strategy

Liquid Death employed a multi-channel marketing strategy that consistently reinforced its rebellious brand identity. Their viral videos, including one featuring a heavy metal song about killing plastic pollution, racked up millions of views. They used humor and irony on social media to engage their audience, creating a loyal following that shared the brand's content.

Even their packaging carried the message: sleek aluminum cans that stood out from plastic bottles. Not only did this align with their environmental mission, but it also communicated a clear difference in product values. Liquid Death's cohesive messaging across various platforms enhanced its influence, effectively connecting with its audience wherever they engaged.

Building an Army of Advocates

Liquid Death transcended traditional advertising methods by transforming its customers into passionate brand ambassadors. They cultivated a community of fans who resonated with its values and humor. Liquid Death empowered its audience to promote its message by providing user-generated content and branded merchandise like T-shirts and hats.

They also partnered with influencers and musicians from alternative scenes, aligning their brand with artists who shared their irreverent ethos. This approach further solidified their connection to a niche but passionate audience, turning casual drinkers into devoted advocates.

Values-Driven Communication

Liquid Death didn't just stand out with humor; they backed it up with a clear mission. Their anti-plastic stance resonated with environmentally conscious consumers, positioning them as a brand with purpose. Campaigns like "Death to Plastic" were effective, as the company donated part of its proceeds to environmental charities.

This alignment between the message and values went beyond mere marketing jargon. It built trust and loyalty among its audience, proving that Liquid Death is more than just a beverage company; it genuinely cares about making a difference.

The Outcome: A Growing Movement

Liquid Death has emerged as a powerful contender in the beverage industry, boasting a valuation exceeding $700 million and making its presence felt in major retailers such as Target and Whole Foods. They didn't just sell water. They sold rebellion, humor, and a shared identity—crushing competitors with clarity and culture. Their ability to connect deeply with their audience has transformed them from a niche product into a cultural phenomenon.

How to Build Your Army of Advocates:

- ✅ Identify your most passionate customers
- ✅ Give them tools and reasons to share
- ✅ Recognize and reward their advocacy
- ✅ Let your brand values lead the way

Liquid Death's narrative beautifully illustrates the concepts discussed in Chapter 6: effective communication transcends mere product sales; it fosters a powerful movement. By aligning their message with the values of their audience and showcasing authenticity and humor, Liquid Death demonstrated that even in saturated markets, a small contender can triumph over giants. Their journey reminds us that when you communicate with purpose, clarity, and boldness, the possibilities are endless.

Liquid Death didn't just market a product—they deployed a narrative. They didn't just gain customers—they built a tribe. That's the power of bold, values-aligned communication in action.

Chapter 6 Key Takeaways: COMMUNICATE—Commanding Attention in the Noise

"Marketing is about commanding the narrative. If you're not clear, your competitors will write it for you."
—Kevin McGrew

KEY LEARNING POINTS

- **The War for Attention: Why Most Messages Fail**

Your market is drowning in noise. Your audience is bombarded with **thousands** of ads, emails, and social posts every day.

Most businesses make the fatal mistake of **blending in**—vague messaging, forgettable branding, and zero differentiation.

If your message isn't clear, compelling, and **impossible to ignore**, you've already lost the battle.

- **The Three Laws of Powerful Communication**

To cut through the clutter and dominate your market, your messaging must be:

- **CLEAR** – If people don't "get it" in seconds, they won't care.

- **CONCISE** – Get to the point. No fluff. No wasted words.

- **COMPELLING** – Make them feel something. Emotion drives action.

- **The Power of Storytelling in Marketing Warfare**

People don't buy products—they buy **stories.**

- Your brand isn't about **what** you sell—it's about **why** it matters.

- Frame your customer as the **hero** and your brand as the **guide.**

- ✅ Use stories of **real people, real struggles, and real victories** to build trust.

- ✅ Make your message personal—**people connect with people, not faceless brands.**

◆ **Your Message Must Be Designed for Combat**

Think of your marketing like a **military transmission**—it must be **short, clear, and impossible to misunderstand.**

✓ **Cluttered messaging? Cut it.**

✓ **Too many value propositions? Pick one.**

✓ **Long-winded explanations? Make it punchy.**

✓ **Confusing brand voice? Simplify it.**

◆ **Mastering the Art of Repetition**

Winning brands repeat their message **until their audience can say it back to them.**

- ✅ Say it again.

- ✅ Say it in a different way.

- ✅ Say it everywhere—social, email, ads, landing pages.

- ✅ If you feel like you're saying it too much, **you're finally being heard.**

◆ **How to Build a Magnetic Brand Voice**

Your brand should **sound like a person, not a corporate memo.**

If your brand **sounds like a PowerPoint, you've already lost.**

- ✅ Use **conversational language**—no jargon, no corporate-speak.

- ✅ Infuse **emotion and personality** into your messaging.

- ✅ Ask direct questions—engage your audience, don't lecture them.

- ✅ Be bold—**safe messaging is invisible.**

- **The War Is Won by the Businesses That Speak Loud and Clear**

  ✕ If your message isn't crystal clear, people will ignore you.

  ✅ If your brand sounds like everyone else, you'll be forgotten.

  ✅ The brands that **speak with clarity, emotion, and repetition** dominate their market.

Action Steps to Command Attention

  ✅ Review your brand messaging—**is it clear, concise, and compelling?**

  ✅ Rewrite your value proposition in **ten words or less.**

  ✅ Identify **one area where your messaging is too vague** and simplify it.

  ✅ Tell a **customer success story** that showcases transformation.

  ✅ Test your message—ask a stranger to repeat what your business does in one sentence.

Final thought: *"Attention is the new currency. If your message isn't sharp, simple, and memorable, it's dead on arrival. Cut the fluff. Speak with power. And make damn sure your audience remembers you."*

You've learned the framework, now upgrade your arsenal.

Scan for advanced training, templates, and live tactical sessions.

Get The SMAC Upgrade

PART III: ADVANCED OPERATIONS

CHAPTER 7

SPECIAL OPERATIONS — DOMINATE— Owning Your Market Like a Military Commander

"When you are outnumbered, innovate. When you are outspent, outthink."
—Unknown Military Strategist

Mission Brief: CHAPTER 7 – Special Operations: Dominate

When the odds are against you, brute force won't cut it. You win with precision, creativity, and strategy. That's the realm of Special Operations.

Your mission:

Deploy advanced tactics to outmaneuver bigger competitors. From guerrilla marketing to covert market entry, this chapter reveals how to punch above your weight and claim territory others overlook. **Domination isn't about doing more—it's about doing what they won't see coming.**

Welcome to the Special Ops phase of the SMAC Framework—where small forces punch far above their weight using precision, stealth, and creativity. In the world of marketing—where creativity often beats brute force—special operations give you the tactical edge to capture new ground and make an outsized impact. This chapter is dedicated to exploring unconventional tactics that can propel your brand to new heights, even against formidable competition.

Reflecting on my naval background, I remember a specific exercise where we were tasked with simulating a covert mission alongside a larger fleet. Though outgunned, we used stealth and precision to outmaneuver a superior force—and complete the mission.

"This experience taught me that success often lies in the ability to think differently and to execute with surgical precision."

In marketing, special operations reflect this mindset, encouraging you to innovate and engage in strategies that might be overlooked by larger, more rigid competitors.

Special operations in marketing are about making the most of your resources—capitalizing on unique advantages, finding untapped opportunities, and leveraging creative strategies that resonate with your audience. This chapter will guide you through crafting and executing these operations, ensuring your brand stands out in a crowded marketplace.

Think Like a Special Forces Unit:

- Use size as an advantage, not a limitation
- Move with stealth, speed, and precision
- Focus on impact, not volume

We'll explore the concept of combined arms marketing, where combining your marketing channels creates a force multiplier—amplifying your impact across every front. When all channels fire together—social, email, events, content—you create a force multiplier that no single tactic can match.

Consider the journey of a small tech start-up that successfully integrated online and offline tactics to capture attention in a competitive landscape. By combining digital marketing with experiential events, they created a buzz that resonated with their target market, achieving results that far exceeded their size.

Additionally, we'll delve into guerrilla tactics for market penetration—strategies that capitalize on agility, surprise, and resourcefulness. Guerrilla tactics help you steal attention with bold, low-cost moves that bigger brands won't risk—and rarely see coming.

Finally, we'll examine covert market entry strategies, which allow you to test new markets and ideas quietly and efficiently. They minimize risk, maximize learning, and let you gather intel without tipping off your competition.

It's not the size of your resources that wins the war—it's how you deploy them. Success lies in your ability to execute with creativity, precision, and a willingness to push boundaries.

Prepare to engage with these unconventional strategies as we navigate this chapter, turning special operations into a cornerstone of your strategic execution. When creativity and resourcefulness lead the mission, your brand doesn't just compete—it carves out its own territory.

Welcome to a world where innovation and strategy converge, equipping you with the tools to execute with impact and ingenuity. As we continue through the SMAC Framework, let these insights guide your journey toward marketing mastery and lasting brand success.

Combined Arms Marketing (Multi-Channel Integration)

In the landscape of modern marketing, where the competition is fierce and resources may be limited, the power of combined arms marketing offers a strategic advantage. This approach, inspired by military tactics, involves the seamless integration of various channels and strategies to create a cohesive force that amplifies your brand's message and impact. This section delves into the art of combining diverse marketing efforts to create a force multiplier that can propel your brand beyond the confines of traditional approaches.

In military terms, combined arms means coordinating infantry, air, and naval units for maximum effect. In marketing, it means synchronizing social, email, events, ads, and content so they amplify each other instead of working in silos. When every channel hits the same target with the same message, you create overwhelming force.

Reflecting on my naval experiences, there was a particular exercise that demonstrated the strength of combined arms. We coordinated air, sea, and land forces, each bringing unique capabilities to achieve a unified objective. This synergy allowed us to leverage the strengths of each unit, creating a formidable presence that was greater than the sum of its parts.

In marketing, this translates into integrating various channels—social media, email, content marketing, events—into a single, powerful strategy that engages your audience on multiple fronts.

Combined arms marketing is about creating a harmonious blend of tactics that work together to enhance your brand's reach and resonance. Here's how you can effectively implement this approach to maximize your marketing efforts:

Understand the Synergy of Channels

The foundation of combined arms marketing is understanding how different channels complement and enhance each other. Each platform has its unique strengths—social media can provide immediacy and interaction, email offers personalization, content marketing builds authority, and events create tangible experiences. By identifying how these elements enhance one another, you can craft a cohesive strategy that maximizes your brand's engagement and impact.

Consider a health and wellness brand that successfully combined digital and physical channels by integrating their social media presence with live workshops and webinars. By doing so, they created a seamless experience that engaged their audience both online and offline, reinforcing their message and building a stronger community.

Align Messaging Across Channels

Consistency in messaging is crucial to ensuring that your combined arms strategy is effective. Develop a unified narrative that resonates across all channels, reinforcing your brand's value proposition and key messages. This alignment not only builds brand recognition but also ensures that your audience receives a coherent and consistent experience.

A regional craft brewery exemplified this by aligning their messaging across social media, email newsletters, and tasting events. By maintaining a consistent voice that highlighted their commitment to quality and local sourcing, they created a cohesive brand experience that resonated with beer enthusiasts.

Leverage Data-Driven Insights

Data is an invaluable asset in crafting a combined arms strategy. Utilize analytics to understand audience behavior across different channels, identifying which platforms drive the most engagement and conversions. By leveraging these insights, you can optimize your strategy, prioritizing efforts where they are most effective and refining your approach to maximize impact.

A tech start-up leveraged data-driven insights to refine their combined arms strategy. By analyzing engagement metrics from their digital campaigns, they identified that their audience preferred in-depth educational content, prompting them to integrate webinars and online courses into their marketing efforts, enhancing engagement and brand loyalty.

Create Integrated Campaigns

Develop campaigns that span multiple channels, ensuring that each component reinforces your overall strategy. These integrated campaigns should be designed to guide your audience through a journey, with each touchpoint building on the previous one. By creating a seamless experience, you enhance engagement and drive conversions.

An e-commerce retailer embraced this approach by launching a seasonal campaign that included social media teasers, email promotions, and in-store events. By creating a cohesive narrative that engaged customers at every touchpoint, they drove awareness and sales, maximizing the impact of their efforts.

Foster Cross-Channel Collaboration

Effective combined arms marketing requires collaboration across teams and departments. Encourage cross-functional collaboration, ensuring that marketing, sales, and customer service teams work together to execute a unified strategy. This alignment not only enhances execution but also ensures that every aspect of your brand's communication is integrated and impactful.

A nonprofit organization demonstrated this by fostering collaboration between their marketing and fundraising teams. By aligning their efforts, they created cohesive campaigns that maximized donor engagement, increasing support for their initiatives.

Monitor and Adapt to Feedback

Feedback is an essential component of refining your combined arms strategy. Monitor audience responses across channels, using this feedback to make adjustments and improvements. By remaining responsive to your audience's needs and preferences, you ensure that your strategy remains relevant and effective.

A subscription service embraced this by actively engaging with customers through social media and email. By soliciting feedback and responding to inquiries, they refined their messaging and strengthened their connection with subscribers.

Measure Success Holistically

Evaluate the success of your combined arms strategy by measuring the collective impact of your efforts. Develop key performance indicators (KPIs) that reflect the integrated nature of your campaigns, tracking metrics such as cross-channel engagement, conversion rates, and customer lifetime value. This holistic approach ensures that you capture the full scope of your strategy's impact.

A financial services firm exemplified this by developing KPIs that measured the success of its integrated marketing efforts. By analyzing metrics across digital and traditional channels, they gained a comprehensive understanding of their strategy's impact, informing future decisions and optimizations.

Combined arms marketing is about orchestrating your efforts to create a symphony of engagement that captivates your audience and reinforces your brand. By integrating diverse tactics into a unified strategy, you amplify your message and maximize your brand's presence, turning your marketing efforts into a powerful force for growth.

As we continue exploring the SMAC Framework, remember that innovation and creativity are at the heart of special operations. With a commitment to combined arms marketing, you ensure that your brand's voice is heard across every platform, resonating with your audience and driving meaningful impact.

Prepare to leverage these insights as you advance through the SMAC Framework, turning combined arms marketing into a cornerstone of your strategic execution. With a cohesive and integrated approach, you navigate the complexities of the market with confidence, ensuring your brand thrives amidst the noise and captures the hearts of your audience.

Guerrilla Tactics for Market Penetration

Guerrilla Marketing Tactics:

- Pop-ups, micro-events, viral contests
- Street-smart content and surprise hooks
- Budget-conscious campaigns that go big on impact

In the realm of marketing, the agility and cunning of guerrilla tactics can offer businesses an edge when resources are limited but ambition is boundless. These tactics, characterized by their unconventional and surprising nature, allow brands to make a significant impact without the need for vast budgets. This section delves into the art of guerrilla marketing, exploring how creativity and strategic thinking can penetrate markets and capture attention in ways that larger, more established brands might overlook.

Reflecting on my experiences, I recall a training exercise where we simulated unexpected engagements, utilizing guerrilla tactics to outsmart a larger force. Our success lies in the element of surprise and our ability to adapt quickly to changing conditions. This taught me the power of thinking outside the box, leveraging creativity over brute force to achieve our objectives. In the business world, guerrilla marketing embodies this philosophy, allowing brands to captivate audiences through innovative, low-cost strategies.

Guerrilla tactics are about leveraging creativity and resourcefulness to create unforgettable brand interactions. Here's how you can harness these strategies to penetrate markets and make a lasting impression:

Embrace the Element of Surprise

Surprise is a powerful tool for capturing attention and engaging audiences. Guerrilla marketing often involves unexpected and unconventional tactics that disrupt the norm and provoke curiosity. By breaking away from traditional marketing approaches, you create memorable experiences that stand out in consumers' minds.

Consider a local coffee shop that transformed an ordinary city corner into a pop-up garden, complete with greenery and free samples. This unexpected gesture not only attracted curious passersby but also created a buzz on social media, extending their reach far beyond the immediate vicinity.

Leverage Local and Community Opportunities

Guerrilla tactics thrive on local engagement and community involvement. Identify opportunities to connect with your audience where they live, work, and play. By embedding your brand within the fabric of the community, you build authentic connections that foster loyalty and advocacy.

A regional gym chain exemplified this by hosting free outdoor fitness classes in local parks. These classes not only attracted fitness enthusiasts but also showcased their community involvement and commitment to health, enhancing their brand reputation and visibility.

Utilize Creative Visuals and Installations

Visual impact is a key component of guerrilla marketing. Use creative visuals and installations to capture attention and convey your brand message in a compelling way. Street art, flash mobs, and interactive displays are just a few examples of how visual elements can create buzz and drive engagement.

An art supply store demonstrated this by commissioning a local artist to create a large, eye-catching mural on their building. This not only drew foot traffic but also became a popular backdrop for social media photos, organically amplifying their brand through user-generated content.

Engage in Tactical Collaborations

Partnerships with complementary businesses can amplify the impact of your guerrilla efforts. Collaborate on joint campaigns or events that leverage each partner's strengths and resources. By pooling your capabilities, you create a more substantial and compelling brand presence.

A boutique bakery and a local bookstore collaborated to host themed book-and-dessert nights. These events attracted a diverse audience, merging the worlds of literature and culinary delight, and creating a unique experience that resonated with both customer bases.

Harness the Power of Storytelling

Storytelling is at the heart of effective guerrilla marketing. Craft a compelling narrative that speaks to your audience's emotions and aspirations. By creating a story that resonates, you inspire engagement and encourage customers to share their experiences with others.

A small outdoor gear retailer embraced storytelling by launching a campaign that highlighted customer adventures and experiences with their products. By sharing these authentic narratives through blogs and social media, they cultivated a community of storytellers who championed their brand.

Utilize Digital Amplification Channels

While guerrilla tactics often start offline, digital amplification can extend their reach exponentially. Use social media, video content, and online communities to share and amplify your guerrilla marketing efforts. This digital component ensures that the impact of your tactics is not confined to a single location or moment.

A grassroots environmental campaign demonstrated this by creating a series of impactful public art installations. By documenting the process and sharing it online, they engaged a global audience, sparking conversations around their cause and driving digital activism.

Measure and Adapt for Success

As with any marketing strategy, measuring the success of guerrilla tactics is essential for refining your approach. Track metrics such as engagement, reach, and conversion rates to assess the impact of your efforts. Use these insights to adapt and optimize future campaigns, ensuring continued success and innovation.

A local pet adoption center exemplified this by tracking the effectiveness of their guerrilla campaigns in increasing adoption rates. By analyzing which strategies generated the most interest, they refined their approach, focusing on tactics that delivered the highest returns.

Guerrilla marketing is about more than just creating noise; it's about crafting memorable experiences that resonate with your audience and leave a lasting impression. By embracing creativity and resourcefulness, you penetrate markets with strategies that captivate and engage, turning curiosity into connection and awareness into advocacy.

As we continue through the SMAC Framework, remember that the heart of guerrilla tactics lies in the willingness to innovate and experiment. With a commitment to creative and unconventional strategies, you ensure that your brand stands out amidst the noise, capturing the attention and imagination of your audience.

Prepare to leverage these insights as you advance through the SMAC Framework, turning guerrilla tactics into a powerful driver of brand impact. With a focus on creativity and agility, you navigate the complexities of the market with confidence, ensuring your brand thrives in even the most competitive environments.

Covert Market Entry Strategies

As we bring our exploration of special operations to a close, we turn our focus to the art of covert market entry strategies. These strategies allow businesses to quietly and efficiently test new markets and ideas, minimizing risk while gathering critical insights. In a world where competition is fierce and the stakes are high, the ability to enter new territories with stealth and precision can be a game-changer. This section delves into how you can deploy covert strategies to expand your reach and inform strategic decisions, ensuring your brand's growth and adaptability in an ever-changing landscape.

"Not every launch should be loud. The best strategies often start in the shadows."

Reflecting on my naval experiences, I recall an exercise that involved infiltrating a heavily guarded area without detection. The mission required meticulous planning, subtlety, and a deep understanding of the terrain. By moving quietly and strategically, we gathered invaluable intelligence that informed future operations, demonstrating the power of stealth and precision. In marketing, covert strategies embody this approach, allowing you to test, learn, and adapt without drawing unnecessary attention or expending excessive resources.

Covert market entry is about entering new spaces with calculated intent, gathering insights that guide your strategic evolution. Here's how you can implement these strategies to expand your reach and enhance your brand's impact:

Conduct Thorough Market Research

Before entering a new market, conduct comprehensive research to understand the landscape. Analyze consumer behaviors, cultural nuances, and competitive dynamics to identify opportunities and potential challenges. This research provides the foundation for informed decision-making, ensuring that your entry is strategic and calculated.

Consider a small tech firm that sought to expand into international markets. By conducting in-depth research into local technology adoption and consumer preferences, they tailored their offerings to meet specific regional needs, enhancing their chances of success.

Test with Pilot Programs

Pilot programs offer a low-risk way to test new ideas and markets. Launch small-scale initiatives that allow you to gather data and assess feasibility without committing significant resources. By evaluating the results of these pilots, you can refine your approach and scale successful strategies with confidence.

An independent film studio exemplified this by releasing a limited edition of their latest project at select film festivals before a broader release. The pilot screenings provided valuable feedback and insights, helping them refine their marketing and distribution strategies for a wider audience.

Leverage Local Partnerships

Local partnerships can facilitate a smooth market entry by providing access to established networks and expertise. Collaborate with companies or influencers who share your values and can amplify your efforts. These partnerships enhance credibility and ensure that your brand resonates with local audiences.

A regional food brand demonstrated this by partnering with local restaurants to introduce their products. By leveraging the reputation and reach of their partners, they increased brand visibility and built trust within the community, paving the way for successful market entry.

Implement Stealth Marketing Techniques

Stealth marketing involves subtle tactics that promote your brand without overt advertising. Utilize approaches such as influencer collaborations, product placements, and organic content to create buzz and awareness.

By engaging audiences organically, you build intrigue and interest without drawing excessive attention.

A boutique fashion retailer embraced this by collaborating with popular lifestyle bloggers to feature their products in organic, everyday settings. This approach generated authentic interest and engagement, attracting new customers to their brand.

Gather and Analyze Feedback

Feedback is crucial for validating market entry strategies and informing future decisions. Use surveys, focus groups, and social listening to gather insights from your audience. Analyze this feedback to understand what resonates and what requires adjustment, ensuring your approach remains aligned with market expectations.

A subscription box service utilized this by conducting post-launch surveys with initial customers. The feedback they received helped them refine their offerings and marketing messages, leading to improved customer satisfaction and increased retention rates.

Maintain a Flexible Approach

Flexibility is key to navigating new markets successfully. Be prepared to adapt your strategies based on real-time insights and changing market conditions. By remaining agile, you ensure that your brand remains relevant and responsive to new opportunities and challenges.

A healthcare start-up illustrated this by adapting their telehealth platform to meet varying regulatory requirements in different regions. Their flexibility allowed them to scale effectively and meet the needs of diverse markets.

Measure Success and Plan for Scale

Evaluate the success of your covert market entry strategies by tracking key performance indicators (KPIs) such as engagement, conversions, and market penetration. Use these insights to plan for scaling successful strategies, ensuring that your brand's growth is sustainable and informed.

A digital marketing agency demonstrated this by analyzing the results of their regional campaigns before launching nationwide. By assessing the effectiveness of their tactics, they optimized their approach for broader implementation, ensuring a successful expansion.

Know When the Mission Is Working:

- Track engagement and conversion impact

- Watch cost per impression and viral spread

- Adapt based on real-time field data

Covert market entry strategies empower your brand to explore new territories with stealth and precision, gathering insights that drive informed growth and adaptation. By entering new markets quietly and strategically, you minimize risk while maximizing learning, setting the stage for successful expansion.

As we conclude this chapter on special operations, remember that the power of innovation lies in your ability to think creatively and act strategically. With a commitment to unconventional approaches, you ensure that your brand remains competitive and adaptable in a rapidly changing marketplace.

Prepare to leverage these insights as you advance through the SMAC Framework, turning covert market entry into a cornerstone of your strategic execution. With stealth and precision as your guiding principles, you navigate the complexities of the market with confidence, ensuring your brand thrives amidst the noise and captures the hearts of your audience.

Remember, you don't need to match your competitor's budget. You need to outthink them, outmaneuver them, and execute like a SEAL team. In marketing warfare, special ops aren't optional—they're how you win when the odds are stacked against you.

"Special operations aren't the backup plan.
They're how underdogs win."

Real-World Case Study: Oatly—Guerrilla Tactics to Disrupt the Dairy Industry

For decades, the dairy industry dominated the beverage aisle, with powerful marketing campaigns from Goliaths like Dairy Farmers of America and multinational corporations pushing milk as a daily staple. In this space, plant-based alternatives were niche products relegated to health-food stores and specialty sections. Then came Oatly, a Swedish oat milk company founded in the 1990s, which skyrocketed to global prominence by 2014. Armed with quirky guerrilla tactics, a mission-driven brand, and a bold refusal to conform, Oatly transformed from a little-known alternative into a household name.

Combined Arms Marketing: Multi-Channel Integration

Oatly didn't rely on traditional advertising methods to break into the U.S. and European markets. Instead, they used a combination of provocative outdoor ads, humorous digital content, and strategic in-store partnerships to amplify their message.

Their billboards and subway ads didn't just sell oat milk—they challenged the status quo with slogans like *"It's like milk but made for humans"* and *"Wow, no cow."* These messages weren't just clever; they were conversation starters. By combining these physical campaigns with engaging social media posts and influencer partnerships, Oatly created an ecosystem where their quirky messaging reached consumers on every platform.

Guerrilla Tactics for Market Penetration

Oatly embraced guerrilla-style marketing that played to their strengths as a small, nimble company. In markets dominated by dairy giants, they ran ads with self-deprecating humor, like "We're sorry if we've made you spill your coffee" alongside cheeky disclaimers acknowledging their modest beginnings.

In one notable campaign, they launched *"The Oatly Department of Mind Control,"* a satirical initiative designed to poke fun at their own marketing efforts while creating buzz. These unconventional tactics made Oatly impossible to ignore, positioning them as a fun, irreverent alternative to the polished (and often impersonal) branding of traditional dairy companies.

Covert Market Entry Strategies

Oatly's approach to entering new markets wasn't about flashy launches—it was about embedding itself in the culture. For example, in the U.S., they focused on getting Oatly into independent coffee shops, where baristas became informal ambassadors for the brand. Their oat milk's creamy texture was ideal for lattes and cappuccinos, making it a hit with coffee aficionados.

By targeting coffee shops instead of grocery stores first, Oatly built credibility and word-of-mouth buzz among influencers and trendsetters. This grassroots strategy allowed them to enter the competitive dairy-alternative market quietly but effectively, creating demand before they even hit supermarket shelves.

Mission-Driven Advocacy

Oatly's rise wasn't just about clever ads—it was rooted in a strong environmental mission. They positioned themselves as a sustainable alternative to traditional dairy, emphasizing the environmental impact of oat milk versus cow's milk. Campaigns like *"Help Dad Stop Drinking Milk"* humorously tackled generational habits while subtly reinforcing Oatly's commitment to reducing greenhouse gas emissions.

Their transparency about sustainability efforts further deepened their connection with environmentally conscious consumers. For example, Oatly prominently displays the carbon footprint of their products on their packaging, turning what could be a dry statistic into a point of pride.

The Outcome: A Cultural and Market Force

Oatly's unconventional tactics have paid off in spades. As of 2023, the company operates in over 20 countries and has an estimated valuation of $10 billion. They've become a leading name in the dairy-alternative market, competing with giants like Almond Breeze and Silk while maintaining their distinct, irreverent voice.

Oatly's success highlights the principles in Chapter 7: winning the marketing war doesn't always require traditional firepower. By leveraging multi-channel strategies, guerrilla marketing, and grassroots advocacy, they turned their size and agility into an advantage. Oatly didn't just challenge the dairy industry—they redefined it, proving that a creative, mission-driven approach can carve out space even in the most crowded markets.

For readers inspired by Oatly's journey, their story is a reminder that unconventional methods, when executed with clarity and conviction, can be the ultimate tool for outmaneuvering industry giants.

Chapter 7 Key Takeaways: SPECIAL OPERATIONS — When You Can't Outspend Them, Outsmart Them

"Appear weak when you are strong, and strong when you are weak."
—Sun Tzu, *The Art of War*

KEY LEARNING POINTS

Think Like a Special Forces Unit

Special operations in marketing are about **precision, creativity, and using your size as an advantage—not a weakness.**

In a noisy, oversaturated market, you don't win with brute force. You win with **agility, stealth, and strategic strikes.**

1. Combined Arms Marketing – Maximum Impact, Minimal Waste

- Integrate multiple marketing channels into one **cohesive assault plan**.

- Coordinate timing, messaging, and strategy across platforms— **social media, email, events, direct outreach, and content**—to hit your target from every angle.

- Example: A local gym syncs digital ads, Instagram content, live workouts, and email check-ins into one focused "New Year" campaign for exponential results.

Tactic: Plan your campaigns like a military operation—each channel is a weapon in your arsenal. **When fired together, they amplify each other.**

2. Guerrilla Marketing – Hit Hard Without a Big Budget

- Unconventional tactics = **memorable results.**

- Use surprise, creativity, and community engagement to drive buzz.

⊘ Real-World Win: A start-up hit 1M+ impressions using a $5K budget by running a contest, micro-influencer collabs, and QR-coded packaging.

Tactic: Think street-smart. Pop-ups, contests, viral hooks, and localized stunts are your battlefield tricks. Guerrilla wins happen when **you stop playing it safe.**

3. Covert Market Entry—Quietly Capture Enemy Territory

⊘ Not every launch should be loud. Test markets **under the radar** to learn and refine before going wide.

⊘ Use **soft launches, micro-campaigns, and partnerships** to sneak into a space and build a presence before competitors notice.

⊘ Oatly's U.S. strategy? Baristas first, supermarkets second. Genius.

Tactic: Treat new markets like reconnaissance missions—**observe, test, gather feedback, then scale.**

4. Special Ops Metrics—Know When the Mission Is Working

⊘ Track engagement, conversion impact, cost efficiency, brand lift, and community growth.

⊘ Learn from the field. Measure and adapt in real time.

⊘ Don't just deploy tactics—**evaluate what moves the needle.**

Action Steps to Deploy Your Special Ops Unit

⊘ Map your current channels—where can you create synergy?

⊘ Identify 2-3 guerrilla ideas you can launch on a shoestring.

⊘ Choose one market to test a covert launch strategy.

⊘ Measure success with KPIs like impressions, engagement, and conversion, **not vanity metrics.**

Final thought: *"You don't need to match your competitor's budget. You need to outthink them, outmaneuver them, and execute like a SEAL team. In marketing warfare, special ops aren't optional—they're how you win when the odds are stacked against you."*

CHAPTER 8

Securing the Victory

"Success is the result of perfection, hard work, learning from failure, loyalty, and persistence."
— Gen. Colin Powell

Mission Brief: CHAPTER 8 – Securing The Victory: Building Your Marketing Special Forces

Winning a battle is one thing. Holding the ground—and expanding your reach—is another. Victory is secured by disciplined teams who can operate independently, adapt under pressure, and execute with precision.

Your mission:

Build a lean, agile, and highly trained marketing unit. This chapter shows you how to structure your team like a Special Forces squad— small, elite, and deadly effective. Because scaling isn't about adding more people—it's about training the right people to fight smarter, faster, and together.

This final chapter is about securing lasting victory—not just the win, but the systems and teams that keep you winning. Victory doesn't end at the win—it's secured by teams built to adapt, innovate, and lead. This chapter is about building that force. In a world where markets are in constant flux, the ability to survive and thrive is the hallmark of a truly successful strategy. Winning the battle is one thing—holding the ground is another. That's where Special Forces come in.

Reflecting on my naval experiences, building a versatile and responsive team was paramount. Success wasn't about firepower—it was about people. Strategy. Execution.

These teams were our special forces, equipped to handle diverse scenarios with precision and expertise. In marketing, your special forces are the strategic systems and teams that drive your brand forward, no matter what the market throws your way.

Mini-Case: How Gymshark Built a Lean, Elite Team That Outgrew the Giants

When Gymshark started in a garage in the UK, they weren't just outgunned—they were out-funded, out-known, and out-resourced by the likes of Nike and Adidas. But founder Ben Francis didn't try to mimic the big brands. He built a small, in-house squad of high-skill operators who understood the digital battlefield.

Instead of bloated layers of bureaucracy, Gymshark's team moved like a special ops unit:

- Creators embedded inside the brand were given real-time freedom to test, post, and iterate.

- Their media team responded to cultural trends in hours, not weeks.

- They used influencer relationships like force multipliers—treating content creators as extensions of the brand, not just ad space.

They didn't need 200 people. They needed 20 trained, aligned, and empowered operators.

The result? From zero to a $1.45 billion valuation in under a decade—without ever raising VC money until much later. Their Marketing Special Forces helped them own their niche, build a global following, and punch far above their weight class.

Lesson: Big teams don't win. Trained ones do.

This chapter will guide you through constructing and nurturing these special forces, ensuring they are equipped to secure your brand's enduring success. We'll explore how to build systems that not only support current objectives but also scale and adapt as your business grows.

We'll begin by examining how to develop a commander's strategic playbook—a comprehensive guide that aligns your marketing efforts with overarching business goals. This playbook ensures every team member understands their role and responsibility—and works cohesively toward common objectives.

Consider a mid-sized company that thrived by implementing a strategic playbook that outlined their marketing objectives and methods, ensuring alignment across all departments. This holistic approach allowed them to respond confidently to market shifts and maintain a consistent brand message.

Additionally, we'll delve into future combat operations, exploring emerging technologies and trends that will shape the landscape of marketing in the years to come. By staying informed and ready to integrate new tools and techniques, you ensure that your brand remains at the forefront of innovation.

Success that lasts isn't luck—it's built on preparation and adaptability. By cultivating a marketing special forces team, you ensure your brand is equipped to navigate uncertainty and seize opportunities with agility and precision.

The SMAC Framework wasn't just a strategy. It's your new doctrine. Apply it, refine it, own it. With a focus on resilience and innovation, you ensure that your brand is well-equipped to thrive in the dynamic landscape of modern marketing.

Welcome to this final exploration, where preparation and foresight converge to secure your brand's future. As we conclude this journey through the SMAC Framework, let these insights guide your path toward marketing mastery and enduring success.

"Victory is not a campaign—it's a commitment."

Building Your Marketing Special Forces

Marketing Special Forces Playbook:

- Train for speed, precision, and resilience
- Establish performance standards
- Scale systems as you grow
- Don't just hire marketers—build operators

As we delve into the final phase of the SMAC Framework, our focus turns to constructing a strategic playbook—a vital tool that serves as the backbone of your marketing special forces. This isn't a binder—it's a battlefield blueprint. A tool to align every team member toward a single mission.

Your playbook keeps everyone aligned, executing with clarity, purpose, and precision.

Reflecting on my past experiences, I recall a time when the importance of a well-crafted plan became crystal clear. On a mission that required precise coordination across multiple units, having a detailed operational plan was crucial. This plan served as our strategic playbook, outlining roles, timelines, and objectives, ensuring that everyone was on the same page.

> *"The difference between temporary success and lasting victory lies in the systems you build and the people you develop."*

In marketing, a strategic playbook provides the same clarity, guiding your team through the complexities of execution while maintaining focus on the bigger picture. Building a strategic playbook involves several key components that collectively ensure its effectiveness as a guiding tool for your marketing efforts:

Define Clear Objectives and Metrics

The foundation of any strategic playbook is a set of clear and measurable objectives that align with your business goals. These objectives should be specific, attainable, and time-bound, providing a roadmap for your marketing efforts. Additionally, identify key metrics that will measure success, allowing you to track progress and make informed adjustments as needed.

Consider a regional retailer that defined objectives centered around increasing online sales and expanding its customer base. By identifying metrics such as website traffic, conversion rates, and customer acquisition cost, they created a framework for measuring success and guiding their marketing efforts.

Establish Roles and Responsibilities

Clarity in roles and responsibilities is crucial for effective execution. Clearly outline the tasks and expectations for each team member, ensuring that everyone understands their contributions to the overall strategy. This alignment fosters collaboration and accountability, ensuring your team functions as a cohesive unit.

A tech start-up exemplified this by creating detailed role descriptions within their marketing playbook. By defining responsibilities for content creation, social media management, and analytics, they ensured that their team operated efficiently and effectively, maximizing productivity and impact.

Develop a Messaging Framework

A consistent and compelling message is key to resonating with your audience. Develop a messaging framework that articulates your brand's value proposition, key messages, and tone of voice. This framework ensures that all communications align with your brand's identity, reinforcing your message across all channels and touchpoints.

An educational institution embraced this by crafting a messaging framework that highlighted its commitment to student success and innovation. By maintaining this consistency across marketing materials, it strengthened its brand identity and attracted prospective students who shared its values.

Outline Tactical Plans

Each objective within your strategic playbook should have a corresponding tactical plan that outlines the specific actions required to achieve it. These plans should include timelines, budgets, and resources needed, providing a clear roadmap for execution. By detailing tactical plans, you ensure that your strategy is actionable and that your team is prepared to implement it effectively.

A nonprofit organization demonstrated this by developing tactical plans for its fundraising initiatives. By outlining the steps involved in donor outreach, event planning, and campaign execution, they ensured that their efforts were organized and impactful, driving support for their mission.

Integrate Feedback Mechanisms

Feedback is an essential component of continuous improvement. Incorporate mechanisms for gathering feedback from team members, stakeholders, and external sources. Use this feedback to refine your strategy, making adjustments that enhance effectiveness and drive better outcomes.

A healthcare provider illustrated this by including regular feedback sessions in their strategic playbook. By soliciting input from staff and patients, they identified areas for improvement in their marketing approach, leading to more targeted and effective communications.

Plan for Contingencies

The market is dynamic, and unforeseen challenges are inevitable. Include contingency plans within your playbook to address potential obstacles and changes in the market. These plans provide a safety net, ensuring that your team is prepared to adapt and respond quickly to disruptions.

A financial services firm demonstrated this by incorporating contingency plans for economic downturns within its strategic playbook. By outlining alternative strategies for maintaining customer engagement and retention, they ensured resilience in challenging times.

Foster a Culture of Collaboration

A successful strategic playbook is driven by a culture of collaboration and open communication. Encourage team members to share ideas, insights, and feedback, fostering an environment where innovation and creativity thrive. This collaborative culture ensures your strategy remains dynamic and responsive to new opportunities.

A regional publishing company embraced this by hosting regular strategy workshops, where team members from various departments collaborated on marketing initiatives. This approach not only fostered creativity but also ensured that diverse perspectives informed their strategy, enhancing overall effectiveness.

The strategic playbook is more than just a plan; it is a living document that guides your marketing efforts, aligning them with your brand's vision and goals. By developing a comprehensive and flexible playbook, you provide your team with the clarity and direction to execute effectively, ensuring that your marketing efforts drive sustained success.

As we continue through the SMAC Framework, remember that preparation and foresight are the cornerstones of enduring success. With a strategic playbook as your guiding tool, you ensure your brand remains agile, adaptable, and ready to seize opportunities in a real-time battlefield.

Prepare to leverage these insights as you advance through the SMAC Framework, turning your strategic playbook into a powerful driver of brand impact. With a focus on alignment and execution, you navigate the complexities of the market with confidence, ensuring your brand thrives amidst the noise and captures the hearts of your audience.

The Commander's Strategic Playbook

As we delve deeper into this final chapter of the SMAC Framework, our focus shifts to future combat operations—the strategies and technologies that will shape the marketing landscape of tomorrow.

The world of marketing is rapidly evolving, with new tools and trends continually emerging. By staying informed and ready to integrate these advancements, you ensure that your brand remains at the forefront of innovation, poised to capitalize on the opportunities that lie ahead.

> *"A documented system becomes your*
> *repeatable engine of success."*

Reflecting on my experiences, I recall a training exercise where we were introduced to the latest advancements in naval technology. The ability to adapt and incorporate these innovations into our operations was crucial for maintaining our competitive edge. In marketing, embracing emerging technologies and trends is similarly essential for staying ahead of the competition and delivering impactful results.

Future combat operations in marketing involve recognizing and integrating the tools and strategies that will drive growth and differentiation in the years to come. Here's how you can prepare your brand to navigate the future landscape and secure enduring success:

Embrace Artificial Intelligence and Automation

Artificial intelligence (AI) and automation are transforming how marketers engage with audiences. These technologies offer the potential to enhance efficiency, personalize experiences, and optimize decision-making. By leveraging AI and automation, you can streamline processes, improve targeting accuracy, and deliver more relevant content to your audience.

Consider a retail brand that integrated AI-driven chatbots into its customer service operations. These chatbots provided instant support and personalized recommendations, improving customer satisfaction and reducing response times. By embracing automation, they enhanced the customer experience and freed up human agents to focus on more complex inquiries.

Explore Augmented Reality and Virtual Reality

Augmented reality (AR) and virtual reality (VR) offer immersive experiences that engage audiences in new and exciting ways. These technologies create opportunities to showcase products, tell stories, and connect with customers on a deeper level. By incorporating AR and VR into your marketing strategy, you can differentiate your brand and create memorable interactions.

A real estate agency exemplified this by using VR to offer virtual property tours. Prospective buyers could explore homes from the comfort of their living rooms, providing a convenient and engaging alternative to traditional viewings. This innovative approach expanded their reach and increased inquiries.

Leverage Data Analytics and Insights

Data is the lifeblood of informed decision-making. As the volume of available data grows, the ability to analyze and interpret it becomes increasingly critical. By leveraging data analytics, you gain insights into consumer behavior, preferences, and trends, informing your strategies and driving more effective marketing efforts.

A tech company embraced data analytics to refine its product development and marketing strategies. By analyzing user data and feedback, they identified areas for improvement and opportunities for innovation, ensuring that their offerings remained aligned with customer needs.

Harness the Power of Social Commerce

Social media platforms are evolving into powerful commerce channels, offering new opportunities for brands to engage with customers and drive sales. By integrating social commerce into your strategy, you can reach customers directly where they spend their time, creating seamless shopping experiences and enhancing brand visibility.

A beauty brand successfully harnessed social commerce by launching exclusive product drops on Instagram. By creating a sense of urgency and exclusivity, they drove engagement and sales, leveraging the platform's reach to expand their customer base.

Stay Informed on Emerging Trends

The marketing landscape is constantly changing, with new trends emerging regularly. Stay informed by following industry publications, attending conferences, and engaging with thought leaders. By staying ahead of the curve, you position your brand to capitalize on new opportunities and remain competitive in a dynamic environment.

A digital agency exemplified this by dedicating resources to trend analysis and innovation. By staying informed on emerging technologies and consumer preferences, they provided cutting-edge solutions that kept their clients ahead of the competition.

Foster a Culture of Innovation

Encourage a culture that values creativity and innovation, empowering your team to explore new ideas and approaches. By fostering an environment where experimentation is encouraged, you ensure that your brand remains adaptable and ready to embrace future advancements.

A tech start-up embraced this by hosting regular innovation workshops where employees could brainstorm and prototype new solutions. This culture of innovation led to the development of groundbreaking products and services that differentiated them in the market.

Prepare for the Future of Privacy and Ethics

As technology advances, issues of privacy and ethics become increasingly important. Prepare for the future by implementing practices that prioritize data security and ethical considerations. By building trust with your audience, you ensure that your brand maintains a positive reputation and fosters long-term loyalty.

A fintech company demonstrated this by adopting transparent data practices and prioritizing user consent. By communicating their commitment to privacy, they built trust with their customers and enhanced their brand's credibility.

Future combat operations in marketing are about more than just adopting new tools—they're about integrating these advancements into a cohesive strategy that drives growth and differentiation. By embracing emerging technologies and trends, you ensure that your brand remains at the forefront of innovation, poised to capitalize on the opportunities that lie ahead.

As we continue through the SMAC Framework, remember that the future belongs to those prepared to adapt and evolve. With a commitment to innovation and foresight, you ensure that your brand remains resilient and competitive, navigating the complexities of the market with confidence and clarity.

Prepare to leverage these insights as you advance through the SMAC Framework, turning future combat operations into a powerful driver of brand impact. With an eye on the horizon and a focus on innovation, you navigate the complexities of the market confidently, ensuring your brand thrives amidst the ever-changing landscape.

Future Combat Operations (Emerging Technologies & Trends)

"The businesses that thrive tomorrow are already training for the fight today."

As we bring this journey through the SMAC Framework to its conclusion, our focus turns to synthesizing the insights we've gathered into a cohesive strategy that secures your brand's enduring success. This final section centers on building a resilient foundation—systems and mindsets that empower your business to not only navigate the present but also anticipate and thrive in the future. By embracing adaptability, innovation, and strategic thinking, you create a brand that's prepared to excel, regardless of what the market may hold.

Reflecting on my time in the Navy, I am reminded of the importance of resilience and adaptability. In a world where conditions can change rapidly and unpredictably, having a strong foundation allows us to face challenges with confidence and poise.

This resilience was cultivated through rigorous training, continuous learning, and a commitment to strategic excellence. In the business world, the same principles apply. A resilient brand not only withstands the test of time but also evolves and grows in the face of change.

As we wrap up this exploration, consider the key elements that form the backbone of a sustainable and future-ready brand:

Cultivate a Learning Organization

Marketing Special Forces Playbook:

- Mission and core beliefs
- Operational checklists
- Decision-making frameworks
- Success metrics and team roles

Continuous learning is at the heart of resilience and adaptability. Foster a culture where team members are encouraged to learn, experiment, and innovate. By investing in training and development, you ensure that your organization remains skilled, informed, and prepared to embrace new challenges and opportunities.

A regional technology company exemplified this by creating a robust professional development program that encouraged employees to pursue certifications and attend industry conferences. This focus on learning not only enhanced their team's capabilities but also ensured that their offerings remained competitive and relevant.

Prioritize Customer-Centric Strategies

The success of any brand hinges on its ability to meet customer needs and exceed expectations. Prioritize customer-centric strategies that place your audience at the core of your decision-making processes. By understanding and anticipating their needs, you build trust and foster lasting relationships that drive loyalty and advocacy.

A healthcare provider embraced this by implementing patient-centered care initiatives that prioritized feedback and personalized experiences. By focusing on their patients' needs, they improved satisfaction and outcomes, reinforcing their reputation for quality care.

Build Flexible and Scalable Systems

Flexibility and scalability are essential for navigating a rapidly changing market. Develop systems and processes that can be easily adapted and scaled as your business grows. This flexibility ensures that your brand remains agile, capable of responding quickly to opportunities and challenges.

A retail chain demonstrated this by implementing a cloud-based inventory management system that allowed them to scale operations efficiently. This adaptability enabled them to expand into new markets seamlessly, ensuring continued growth and success.

Foster Strategic Partnerships

Strategic partnerships can extend your reach and resources, providing access to new markets, expertise, and capabilities. Identify partners whose values and goals align with yours, and collaborate to create mutually beneficial opportunities that drive innovation and growth.

A beverage company illustrated this by partnering with a leading distribution network to expand its product availability. This collaboration not only increased their market presence but also enhanced their brand visibility and credibility.

Encourage a Culture of Innovation

Innovation is the engine of growth and differentiation. Foster a culture where creativity is encouraged, and new ideas are welcomed. By creating an environment where experimentation is valued, you ensure your brand remains at the forefront of innovation, ready to seize emerging opportunities.

A financial services firm embraced this by hosting regular innovation challenges, where employees were encouraged to brainstorm and prototype new solutions. This culture of innovation led to the development of groundbreaking products and services that differentiated them in the market.

Prepare for Future Trends and Challenges

Prepare for Future Combat:

- Assign a team member to track trends monthly
- Build innovation into your systems
- Train your team to adapt before it's urgent

The future is full of possibilities and uncertainties. Prepare for what's ahead by staying informed about emerging trends and potential challenges. By anticipating these changes, you position your brand to capitalize on new opportunities and navigate any obstacles that arise.

An e-commerce platform exemplified this by dedicating resources to trend analysis and strategic foresight. By staying informed on consumer preferences and technological advancements, they provided cutting-edge solutions that kept their clients ahead of the competition.

Measure Success and Continuously Improve

Regularly assess your brand's performance and analyze the outcomes of your strategies. Use key performance indicators (KPIs) to measure success and identify areas for improvement. This commitment to continuous improvement ensures that your brand remains dynamic and responsive, capable of thriving in a changing market.

A nonprofit organization demonstrated this by implementing regular performance reviews and feedback sessions. By analyzing the effectiveness of their initiatives and making data-driven adjustments, they ensured their strategies remained impactful and aligned with their mission.

🎯 Ready to Secure the Victory?

You've read the battle plans. Now it's time to execute.

Introducing AI-First Warfare: The SMAC Operator's Edge — a tactical course designed to help you operationalize everything you've learned in The New Rules of Marketing Warfare using the power of AI.

🔥 Learn to shoot with precision, move fast, adapt smarter, and command with confidence — with AI as your force multiplier.

> Enroll now and start winning the marketing war. The course is $497. Use CODE: SMACAI50 to get 50% off the course. Limited redemptions: First 500 get 50% off - Enlist now!

AI-First Warfare: The SMAC Operator's Edge Course

[Scan the QR Code or visit MarketingWarfareHQ.com/ai-first-course]

Real-World Case Study: Canva—Securing Victory by Democratizing Design

In a world where design was once the domain of professionals armed with expensive tools, Canva emerged as a David who transformed the landscape by empowering the everyday user.

Founded in 2012, Canva set out to democratize design, making it accessible to anyone—small business owners, educators, social media managers, and solopreneurs—regardless of their budget or skill level. Their story illustrates how aligning with user needs, creating scalable systems, and staying true to a vision can secure victory even in an industry dominated by giants like Adobe.

Building Marketing Special Forces: Empowering Users, Not Just Selling Tools

Canva's marketing doesn't simply focus on selling software; it champions creativity and accessibility. Their campaigns are built on the philosophy of empowering users to take control of their visual storytelling, regardless of their design expertise.

For example, Canva's "Design Anything" campaign was a bold statement that redefined what design software could be. Rather than highlighting technical features, Canva showcased real stories of small businesses, teachers, and creators transforming their lives with Canva's easy-to-use tools.

They also leveraged user-generated content, encouraging customers to share their Canva creations on social media. This approach turned users into brand ambassadors and sparked a wave of organic advocacy that significantly expanded their reach.

The Commander's Strategic Playbook: Aligning Business with Mission

From day one, Canva's leadership emphasized a user-first approach. The mission was clear: make design accessible to everyone, everywhere. This clarity allowed Canva to make decisions that balanced short-term wins with long-term sustainability.

By offering a free version of their platform with robust capabilities, Canva ensured they could serve their core audience—small businesses and individuals—while generating revenue through premium plans. This dual model allowed them to grow rapidly without alienating users who couldn't afford traditional software.

Canva's leadership also prioritized accessibility on a global scale. By localizing their platform into over 100 languages and creating culturally relevant templates, they expanded into international markets while maintaining their user-centric ethos.

Future Combat Operations: Preparing for Tomorrow's Creative Needs

Canva's adaptability ensures it remains ahead of industry trends. They've evolved from a simple design tool into a comprehensive creative platform, adding features like video editing, team collaboration tools, and even AI-driven design suggestions.

One of its most innovative moves was the introduction of Canva for Teams, which catered to small businesses looking for an affordable solution to unify their branding across employees. This expansion into team collaboration positioned Canva as a serious competitor to enterprise-focused platforms while staying true to its roots.

Canva also recognized the growing importance of sustainability in branding. By offering templates and tools to help businesses create eco-conscious messaging and campaigns, Canva aligned itself with a future-focused audience that values purpose-driven practices.

The Outcome: A Movement in Design

Today, Canva is more than a tool—it's a movement. With over 125 million monthly active users creating 3 billion designs annually, Canva has redefined who can be a designer. Small businesses that once struggled to create professional visuals now have a level playing field, thanks to Canva's accessible platform.

Their commitment to long-term goals over quick wins has solidified Canva as a trusted partner for creators and businesses alike. More importantly, they've sparked a cultural shift in the way design is perceived and utilized, proving that empowering users is the ultimate key to success.

Lessons from Canva's Journey:

1. **Empower Users:** Canva's success lies in its ability to turn users into advocates. By prioritizing ease of use and accessibility, it created a product that users love to share.

2. **Balance Free and Premium:** Its dual-pricing model ensures it serves its core audience while generating sustainable revenue from power users.

3. **Expand with Purpose:** Canva's localized approach and continual feature expansion show the importance of understanding and addressing evolving customer needs.

4. **Stay Mission-Focused:** Canva's clear mission to democratize design has been its North Star, guiding decisions that build trust and loyalty.

Conclusion:

Canva's journey is a powerful testament to the principles of Chapter 8: achieving victory through sustainable practices, an unwavering focus on user needs, and strategic adaptability. They didn't merely create a product; they transformed the entire industry landscape.

For businesses aiming for lasting success, Canva's story clearly demonstrates that aligning with your audience's needs and remaining steadfast to your mission will secure a unique and enduring position in any market.

You don't have to fight alone. Join the SMAC operator community at MarketingWarfareHQ.com and train with others who *refuse to lose.*

Chapter 8 Key Takeaways:
Securing the Victory

"The difference between temporary success and lasting victory lies in the systems you build and the people you develop."
–Kevin McGrew

KEY LEARNING POINTS

Winning the War Is Just the Beginning

Victory isn't crossing the finish line—it's building a force that can **hold the line, expand territory, and win again tomorrow.**

This chapter is about turning your momentum into a movement.

1. Build Your Marketing Special Forces

- **Develop elite teams** that execute with speed, precision, and purpose.

- Invest in training, performance standards, and systems that **scale as you grow.**

- Don't just hire marketers—**build operators** ready for the next campaign.

Tactic: Conduct a skills audit and plug your gaps with training, mentorship, or strategic hires.

2. Create The Commander's Strategic Playbook

- Document your strategy so your team isn't guessing—it's marching in sync.

- Your playbook includes:

  - Core beliefs and brand mission

  - Operational checklists

  - Decision-making frameworks

⊘ A documented system becomes your **repeatable engine of success**.

Tactic: Start with a one-page SOP for your most effective campaign. Then scale that structure.

3. Prepare for Future Combat Operations

> *"Want to win tomorrow? Prepare today."*

⊘ Stay ahead of trends—**AI, voice search, creator marketing, personalization**—don't wait to react.

⊘ Future-proof your tech, systems, and people.

⊘ The businesses that thrive tomorrow are already **training for the fight today.**

Tactic: Assign one team member to report monthly on emerging tech. Make it a standing agenda item.

Case Study: Canva – Building a Movement, Not Just a Product

Canva didn't just win market share—it changed the entire battlefield.

⊘ Empowered users to become advocates

⊘ Balanced free tools with a smart upsell path

⊘ Expanded with purpose, not hype

⊘ Stayed mission-driven: democratize design for everyone

Lesson: The war is won when your brand becomes a cause others want to join.

Final thought: *"Victory is not a campaign—it's a commitment. It's about training your people, building your systems, and staying focused on your mission, even as the terrain shifts. Want to win tomorrow? Prepare today."*

CHAPTER 9

Building Your Digital Arsenal — Core Platforms and Infrastructure

"He who controls the digital battlefield controls the future."
—Modern Marketing Maxim

Mission Brief: CHAPTER 9 – The Path Forward: Becoming a SMAC Operator

You've learned the tactics. You've seen the strategy. Now it's time to make it your operating system. Because this isn't the end of the mission—it's the beginning of your campaign.

Your mission:

Own the SMAC mindset. Apply it, refine it, and lead with it. Now it's time to embed Shoot, Move, Adapt, and Communicate into the DNA of your business—where strategy becomes standard operating procedure. From this point on, you're not just a marketer. You're a SMAC Marketer—trained to outthink, outmaneuver, and outlast the competition.

In my days aboard the nuclear-powered cruiser USS Long Beach, our ship was more than steel and systems—it was our command center, our base, and our primary force projection platform.

Your digital landscape today isn't much different. The terrain has changed. But the mission? It's the same: reach, influence, and impact. Your digital presence serves the same vital functions: it's your command center, your base of operations, and your primary means of projecting influence across the vast digital seas.

> *"Your website is your command center—your sovereign territory in the vast digital landscape."*

As we've navigated through the SMAC Framework, we've explored how smaller forces can outmaneuver larger competitors through precision, agility, and strategic communication. Now it's time to examine the specific weapons and infrastructure you need in your digital arsenal.

Just as a military force requires the right equipment and bases to operate effectively, your business needs the right digital platforms and infrastructure to compete in today's market.

In my years helping businesses wage and win their marketing battles, I've seen too many companies scatter their resources across dozens of digital platforms without a coherent strategy. It's like trying to fight a war by deploying troops randomly across every possible battlefield—ineffective and wasteful. Instead, we need to approach our digital arsenal with strategic precision, understanding the role and importance of each platform in our overall battle plan.

Consider this chapter your digital armory guide—a strategic blueprint for building and deploying the digital assets you need to compete and win in today's market. We'll explore how to establish your command center, secure your supply lines, and maintain forward operating bases that extend your reach and influence.

Your Digital Command Center: Establishing Home Base

Critical Elements for Your Website:

- Clear mission communication
- Secure infrastructure
- Fast load speed
- Conversion-focused layout
- Intelligence gathering systems

In any military operation, the command center is sacred ground—it's where strategies are formed, orders are issued, and intelligence is gathered. In the digital realm, your website serves as this command center. It's the only piece of digital territory you truly own, your sovereign soil in the vast online landscape.

Think about that for a moment: every other digital platform you use—whether it's Facebook, LinkedIn, or Google—is essentially rented space. You're operating on someone else's territory, subject to their rules and algorithmic whims. Your website, however, is yours. You control the message, the experience, and the data. This isn't just a technical distinction—it's a strategic imperative.

During my time helping businesses compete against larger forces, I've seen countless examples of companies learning this lesson the hard way. One retail client had built their entire presence on Facebook, amassing a significant following. When algorithm changes severely reduced their organic reach, they suddenly found themselves cut off from their audience. It was like having supply lines suddenly severed in the middle of a campaign.

> *"If your marketing lives only on platforms you don't control, you're building on rented land."*

Your website serves several critical functions:

Command and Control

- Establishes your official presence and messaging

- Controls the narrative around your brand

- Provides a stable base for all marketing operations

Think of your website as your flagship—it should be impressive enough to command respect, but, more importantly, it needs to be functional and effective. This means:

- Clear navigation (like well-marked corridors on a ship)

- Strong security (like a well-defended perimeter)

- Efficient performance (like a well-maintained engine room)

- Clear communication capabilities (like reliable communication systems)

Intelligence Gathering

Your website should serve as an intelligence hub, collecting valuable data about:

- Visitor behavior
- Conversion patterns
- Content effectiveness
- Customer journey mapping

Resource Deployment

From your website, you should be able to:

- Deploy marketing campaigns
- Manage customer relationships
- Coordinate across different channels
- Track and measure results

Critical Elements for Your Digital Command Center:

A. Clear Mission Communication

Your website must effectively communicate your:

- **Who:** Your identity and unique value proposition
- **What:** Your products/services and solutions
- **Where:** Your service areas and reach
- **Why:** Your mission and purpose
- **When:** Your availability and response times
- **How:** Your processes and methodologies

B. Secure Infrastructure

Ensure your website has:

- SSL security (https://)
- Regular backups
- Updated software and plugins
- Mobile responsiveness
- Fast loading speeds

C. Communication Systems

Make sure to implement the following:

- Contact forms
- Live chat capabilities (if applicable). Use highly trained AI Chatbots to save money.
- Email signup systems
- Appointment booking tools
- Social proof elements

Supply Lines and Provisions: Generating Website Traffic

Your Two-Front Traffic Strategy:

✅ Organic SEO = long-term supply chain

✅ Paid Ads = rapid deployment force

✅ Use both for sustained growth

In military operations, even the strongest fortress is useless without reliable supply lines. The same holds true for your digital command center—a website without traffic is like a base without supplies. But not all supply lines are created equal, and understanding how to establish and maintain them is crucial for sustainable operations.

During my naval career, we learned that sustainable operations required both long-term supply chain planning and immediate resupply capabilities. In digital marketing, this translates to two primary traffic generation approaches: organic search engine optimization (SEO) and paid advertising.

Let me share a story that illustrates this perfectly. A client in the healthcare technology sector was burning through their budget with paid advertising, treating it as their only supply line. When their funding suddenly tightened, their traffic disappeared overnight. It was like a ship stranded at sea without provisions. We helped them establish a balanced approach using both paid and organic strategies, creating resilience in their traffic generation.

Establishing Sustainable Supply Lines (SEO)

Think of SEO as establishing your sustainable supply lines. Like farming, it requires:

Ground Preparation (Technical SEO)

- Site architecture optimization
- Mobile responsiveness
- Page speed optimization
- XML sitemap creation
- Robots.txt configuration

Planting Seeds (On-Page SEO)

- Keyword research and targeting
- Content optimization
- Meta tag optimization
- Internal linking structure
- User experience enhancement

Regular Maintenance (Content Creation)

- Regular blog posts

- Updated service pages

- Fresh, relevant content

- Resource sections

- Case studies and success stories

Timeline Expectations:

Just as crops take time to grow, SEO typically requires 9-12 months to show significant results. However, once established, it provides consistent, cost-effective traffic.

Rapid Deployment Options (Paid Advertising)

While waiting for organic traffic to develop, paid advertising serves as your immediate supply line. Think of it as purchasing ready-to-use provisions:

Search Engine Marketing (SEM)

- Google Ads and/or Bing Ads

Benefits:

- Immediate visibility

- Highly targeted traffic

- Measurable results

Social Media Advertising

- Meta (Facebook/Instagram)

- LinkedIn (B2B)

- TikTok (younger demographics)

- Pinterest (visual products)

Benefits:

- Precise audience targeting
- Visual engagement
- Rapid testing and optimization

Display and Video Advertising

- Google Display Network
- YouTube Ads
- Adroll Ads
- Rollworks (B2B option)

Benefits:

- Broad reach
- Brand awareness
- Visual storytelling

Forward Operating Bases: Social Media Platforms

In military strategy, forward operating bases extend your reach and influence beyond your main base. Social media platforms serve the same function in your digital strategy. They're not just communication channels—they're strategic outposts that provide social proof, intelligence gathering, and engagement opportunities.

Core Platform Deployment Strategy:

For B2C Operations:

Facebook (3+ billion monthly users)

- **Primary mission:** Community building and broad engagement
- **Key tactics:** Regular updates, community management, customer service

- **Strategic value:** Broad demographic reach, detailed targeting options

Instagram (2+ billion monthly users)

- **Primary mission:** Visual brand building and product showcase

- **Key tactics:** High-quality visuals, Stories, Reels

- **Strategic value:** High engagement, strong product discovery

TikTok

- **Primary mission:** Brand awareness and youth market penetration

- **Key tactics:** Trend participation, authentic content, educational snippets

- **Strategic value:** Viral potential, younger demographic reach

For B2B Operations:

LinkedIn

- **Primary mission:** Professional networking and thought leadership

- **Key tactics:** Industry insights, company updates, employee advocacy

- **Strategic value:** Business decision-maker targeting

YouTube

- **Primary mission:** Educational content and brand authority

- **Key tactics:** How-to videos, product demonstrations, thought leadership

- **Strategic value:** Search engine visibility, detailed content sharing

Secure Communication Channels: Email and SMS Infrastructure

In military operations, secure and reliable communication channels are critical for maintaining contact with allies and coordinating operations. In the digital realm, email and SMS marketing serve as your primary communication channels with your most valuable assets—your customers and prospects.

Think back to my days in the Combat Information Center (CIC). We had multiple communication channels, each serving a specific purpose: general broadcasts, secure direct communications, and emergency alerts. Your digital communication strategy should mirror this approach, using email and SMS strategically for different objectives.

Email Marketing: Your Strategic Communication Network

Email remains one of your most powerful communication tools because:

- You own the contact list.

- Messages can be highly personalized.

- Communication is direct and trackable.

- Content can be comprehensive and detailed.

Essential Email Infrastructure Elements:

List Building Strategy

- Strategic opt-in points throughout your website

- Lead magnet development

- Progressive profiling

- Segmentation capabilities

Campaign Types

- Welcome sequences

- Nurture campaigns

- Promotional messages

- Retention communications

- Re-engagement campaigns

Performance Monitoring

- Open rates

- Click-through rates

- Conversion tracking

- List health metrics

- Engagement scoring

SMS Marketing: Rapid Response Communications

SMS marketing is like your emergency broadcast system—immediate, attention-grabbing, and highly effective. It's particularly crucial for:

- E-commerce businesses

- Appointment-based services

- Time-sensitive promotions

- Critical updates

SMS Best Practices:

Timing and Frequency

- Respect business hours

- Limit frequency to prevent fatigue

- Focus on high-value communications

- Coordinate with email campaigns

Message Types

- Order confirmations

- Shipping updates

- Appointment reminders

- Flash sales

- Special promotions

Compliance and Consent

- Clear opt-in processes

- Easy opt-out options

- Privacy policy adherence

- Data protection measures

Local Territory Control: Dominating Your Geographic Space

"Your Google Business Profile is your local war map—control it, or be invisible."

In naval operations, controlling local waters was often as crucial as projecting power across oceans. For businesses with physical locations, dominating local search results is equally vital. Your Google Business Profile serves as your beacon in local waters, guiding potential customers to your location.

Strategic Local Presence Development:

Google Business Profile Optimization

- Complete and accurate business information

- Regular posts and updates

- Photo and video content
- Q&A management
- Review generation and response strategy

Local Search Dominance

- Local keyword optimization
- Location-specific content
- Local backlink development
- Citation management
- Local event participation

Map Pack Positioning

- Category optimization
- Service area definition
- Location verification
- Local content creation
- Review management strategy

Implementation Checklist: Your Digital Arsenal Audit

- ☐ **Command Center (Website)**
  - ☐ Mobile responsiveness verified
  - ☐ Clear messaging established
  - ☐ Security measures implemented
  - ☐ Analytics properly configured
  - ☐ Conversion tracking set up

- ☐ **Traffic Generation**
  - ☐ SEO foundation established
  - ☐ Paid campaign structure created

- ☐ Content calendar developed
- ☐ Traffic sources diversified
- ☐ ROI tracking implemented

☐ **Social Media Presence**

- ☐ Core platforms identified
- ☐ Content strategy developed
- ☐ Posting schedule established
- ☐ Engagement protocols created
- ☐ Performance metrics defined

☐ **Communication Infrastructure**

- ☐ Email platform selected
- ☐ SMS system integrated
- ☐ Automation flows created
- ☐ Segmentation implemented
- ☐ Compliance verified

☐ **Local Presence**

- ☐ GBP fully optimized
- ☐ Local SEO implemented
- ☐ Review system established
- ☐ Local content created
- ☐ Citation network built

Victory in the digital battlefield requires more than just having these platforms—it requires using them strategically and in concert. Like a well-coordinated military operation, your digital arsenal should work together, each platform supporting and amplifying the others.

The Digital Arsenal Audit:

✅ Website performance optimized

✅ SEO & paid traffic in place

✅ Core social platforms activated

✅ Email/SMS flows running

✅ Local search fully optimized

Remember, in today's marketing warfare, your digital arsenal isn't just a collection of tools—it's your means of projecting force, establishing presence, and ultimately achieving your marketing objectives. Build it thoughtfully, maintain it diligently, and deploy it strategically.

"The businesses that win treat their digital infrastructure like a military operation: planned, precise, and always battle-ready."

The digital battlefield evolves rapidly, but the principles of strategic deployment remain constant. Keep your arsenal updated, your communications clear, and your presence strong. That's how smaller forces can continue to win against larger competitors in the digital age.

Tactical Implementation Guide: Deploying Your Digital Arsenal

Phase 1: Establishing Your Command Center (Your Website)

Objective: Create a fast, clear, and conversion-ready home base for your business online.

THE BRIEFING

When new recruits enter any branch of the military, they don't start with complex maneuvers—they start with the basics. Fundamentals. Repetition. Discipline. Because the best in any field are built on strong foundations.

It's no different in business. Yet **42% of small businesses still haven't deployed the basic digital infrastructure needed to compete**, let alone win. That's not just a gap—it's a vulnerability.

This phase is about building your **Command Center**—your website. It's your digital home base, your control tower, your first line of offense and defense. Every ad, email, post, or campaign should lead back here. If this part isn't solid, nothing else will hold.

By executing this phase, you're putting yourself ahead of nearly half your competition. You're choosing not to just survive—but to prepare to **thrive**.

> *"You must crawl before you can walk. Get this part right, and the rest of the SMAC strategy starts making sense."*

Timeline: 30–90 Days

We'll break this into 3 focused sprints.

First 30 Days – Build the Base

Tasks:

- Choose your website platform (WordPress, Squarespace, or Wix)
- Secure your domain name and hosting
- Install an SSL certificate (this makes your site secure with https://)
- Set up Google Analytics and Google Search Console

Mission-Critical Success Markers:

Your website loads in under 3 seconds

It passes Google's mobile-friendliness test

SSL is active and working

Google Analytics and Search Console are both connected and tracking

---

Next 30 Days – Load the Content

Tasks:

Write and publish your top 5 service or product pages

Create an About page that tells your story and builds trust

Build a Contact page with a clear call-to-action

Add 3–5 customer testimonials (start with what you have, polish later)

Mission-Critical Success Markers:

Each page has at least 300 words

Every page includes a clear CTA

Contact forms send properly

Site navigation works smoothly on mobile

Final 30 Days – Equip for Conversions

Tasks:

- Set up a lead capture form (email or phone submission)
- Build a custom thank-you page for form submissions
- Install a chat or chatbot system (optional but powerful)
- Add an appointment booking system if applicable

Mission-Critical Success Markers:

- Forms successfully collect and store leads
- Thank-you pages are tracking conversions
- Chat system responds reliably
- Booking process works seamlessly

Remember: This phase isn't about perfection. It's about **deployment**. Get your Command Center operational, refine over time, and you'll be better positioned than most businesses who never even lay this foundation.

Phase 2: Securing Your Supply Lines (Traffic)

Objective: Establish steady, reliable streams of traffic—both organic and paid—that deliver prospects to your digital front door.

THE BRIEFING

In any military operation, logistics and supply lines determine whether an army can hold its ground or crumble under pressure. You can have the best base in the world, but if you don't have consistent reinforcements—fuel, food, intel, ammo—you lose.

In business, your supply lines are your **traffic channels**. They keep new prospects flowing in. They power your ability to scale. And yet, most small businesses either ignore traffic generation or gamble with it.

Only 39% of businesses are actively investing in SEO. Even fewer have the patience or process to generate sustained, qualified traffic. That's a massive weakness you don't have to share.

This phase will teach you how to build traffic the right way—from two fronts: **organic** (free but long-term) and **paid** (faster but requires budget discipline).

If you complete this phase, you'll be doing what the majority of businesses never commit to: building a pipeline of consistent, targeted attention.

Timeline: 90 Days for foundational SEO, 30 Days for paid ad testing

You don't need to be everywhere. You need to be **strategic** and **measurable**.

Part A: Organic Supply Lines (SEO)

First 90 Days – Build the Foundation

Tasks:

Submit your sitemap to Google via Search Console

Identify and fix any mobile usability issues

Write compelling page titles and meta descriptions for your core pages

Implement local business schema for visibility in local search

Mission-Critical Success Markers:

- No critical errors in Google Search Console
- Your key pages are indexed by Google
- Your schema passes validation tests (using Google's tool)

Content Deployment Strategy (Ongoing)

Tasks:

- Publish 2–3 blog posts per month targeting relevant keywords or FAQs
- Update and expand key service pages
- Add FAQ sections to your main pages using real customer questions
- Begin building quality backlinks—aim for 2–3 per month

Mission-Critical Success Markers:

- A simple content calendar is followed and executed
- Organic traffic begins to increase month-over-month
- Domain authority gradually improves
- Content is shared and indexed regularly

Part B: Paid Supply Lines (Search Advertising)

30-Day Launch Plan

Tasks:

- Choose 3–5 high-intent keywords your audience is already searching
- Set a daily ad budget ($20–$50 depending on your goals)

- Create 2–3 ad variations to test headlines, offers, and CTAs

- Set up conversion tracking in Google Ads and on your website

Mission-Critical Success Markers:

- Your cost-per-click is below your industry's average

- Your conversion rate is above 2%

- You're tracking return on ad spend (ROAS)

- Your Google Quality Scores are above 7/10

Closing Mission Brief

This phase isn't about becoming an SEO wizard or ad expert overnight. It's about **establishing momentum**. By building real traffic pipelines—while others just hope customers stumble onto their site—you gain a tactical edge.

> *"Traffic isn't just a goal. It's a supply line.*
> *Without it, the war's already lost."*

Phase 3: Building Your Forward Operating Bases (Social Media)

Objective: Build a visible, engaging, and consistent brand presence across the platforms your audience already lives on.

THE BRIEFING

In military strategy, forward operating bases are established in hostile or high-traffic zones. They're agile, well-supplied, and built to expand influence. The same applies to your social media presence.

Today's consumers spend hours a day on platforms like Instagram, Facebook, LinkedIn, TikTok, and YouTube. And yet, most small businesses either post sporadically or use social as an afterthought.

This phase gives you the tools to **position your brand where your audience is already active**, build awareness, and open new engagement channels. Remember: it's not about being everywhere—it's about **showing up with intention.**

> *"By executing this phase, you're not just doing social media. You're turning platforms into permanent digital outposts that grow awareness, trust, and attention—even while you sleep."*

Timeline: 90 Days to set up and engage consistently

This is crawl-walk-run. We're still crawling—but these are the moves that build reach over time.

First 30 Days – Set Up Your Bases

Tasks:

- Create or optimize business profiles on 1–3 core platforms where your audience is active
- Ensure brand consistency (logos, bios, links, tone of voice)
- Fill out all business details: hours, contact info, location, and link to website
- Add action buttons where possible (Book Now, Call, Message, etc.

Mission-Critical Success Markers:

- All profiles are 100% complete and accurate
- Brand visuals and messaging match across platforms
- All links work properly
- Business info is easy to find

Next 30 Days – Start Broadcasting

Tasks:

- Create a simple content calendar (1 post/day or 3–5 per week)
- Develop 30 days of posts using a mix of value (tips, stories, education), promotion, and engagement content
- Use a scheduling tool (Buffer, Later, Meta Business Suite, etc.)
- Start engaging: comment on followers' posts, reply to DMs, and follow key accounts

Mission-Critical Success Markers:

- Publishing consistently on schedule
- Engagement rate above 1% per post
- Follower count begins to grow organically
- Conversations happening with followers

Final 30 Days – Build the Community

Tasks:

- Respond to all comments and DMs within 24 hours
- Repost or share user-generated content (UGC) if available
- Collaborate with a complementary local brand or creator
- Analyze top-performing posts and replicate the format

Mission-Critical Success Markers:

- Response time < 24 hours
- Engagement rate trending upward

- Reach expanding weekly
- One cross-promotional effort launched

Closing Mission Brief

This phase isn't about going viral. It's about building **visible trust**. Your social channels aren't just for promotion—they're digital proof you exist, you care, and you deliver value.

> *"This is where your brand's voice meets the public. And when done right, it becomes one of your most powerful assets for long-term growth."*

Phase 4: Setting Up Communication Systems (Email Marketing)

Objective: Build a direct, ownable line of communication with your audience—so you can nurture leads, build trust, and drive consistent revenue.

THE BRIEFING

Every successful military unit has an unbreakable communication system. Without it, missions fail. Confusion spreads. Targets get missed.

In business, email is that system. It's **direct**, reliable, and doesn't depend on algorithms or rented platforms. While social media is where conversations happen, email is where **conversion happens**.

And yet, most small businesses treat email like an afterthought—or worse, don't use it at all. That's a costly mistake.

This phase is about setting up the basic infrastructure for email marketing—so you can communicate consistently with your customers and leads, build relationships, and generate results.

"If you complete this phase, you'll have one of the most valuable and underused tools in small business: a communication channel you control, that builds revenue while others rely on chance."

Timeline: 60 Days to set up and launch foundational campaigns

Keep it simple. Execute well. This is a foundational layer that pays off fast.

First 30 Days – Build the System

Tasks:

- Choose an email platform (Mailchimp, ConvertKit, ActiveCampaign, etc.)

- Create branded email templates (for newsletters and sequences)

- Set up a welcome email or 3-part welcome sequence

- Import your existing contacts (from customer lists, CRM, spreadsheets, etc.)

Mission-Critical Success Markers:

- Your email list is properly segmented (by source, customer type, etc.)

- Your welcome sequence is active and sending

- Your first email sends successfully

- Open rate is above 20%, click-through rate above 2%

Next 30 Days – Automate and Activate

Tasks:

- Develop a basic monthly newsletter (with 2–3 content sections max)

- Build one automated follow-up sequence (lead magnet, abandoned cart, or service inquiry follow-up)

- Add lead capture forms to your website and thank-you pages

- Implement list hygiene practices (unsubscribe management, inactive cleanup)

Mission-Critical Success Markers:

- Newsletter sends on schedule

- Automation is active and running

- Subscriber list grows weekly

- Deliverability is healthy and improving

Closing Mission Brief

This isn't about building a complex funnel. It's about opening a clear, consistent line to your future customers. When used properly, email marketing **pays for itself and becomes a central weapon in your digital arsenal**.

> *"Every campaign starts with attention. But relationships—
> and revenue—are built through communication.
> This is how you scale trust."*

Final Phase: Monthly Maintenance Checklist

Objective: Keep your digital arsenal sharp, operational, and ready to adapt with changing conditions.

THE BRIEFING

In any successful military operation, gear is maintained, plans are reviewed, and systems are inspected regularly. Maintenance is what keeps a fighting force mission-ready.

Your business is no different. This checklist gives you a repeatable, lightweight rhythm to **monitor, refine, and optimize** your marketing infrastructure each month—without overwhelm.

You don't need to overhaul your strategy every 30 days. But you do need to **check the pulse**, fix what's broken, and double down on what's working.

"Most businesses lose momentum because they fail to maintain what they've built. This checklist ensures you stay in motion—and stay in control."

Area	What to Check	Why It Matters
Website	- Test all forms and links - Update service or product info - Check mobile experience - Monitor Google Analytics	Keeps your site usable, fast, and conversion-focused.
Traffic	- Review keyword rankings - Audit Google Ads performance - Adjust bids, budgets, and ad copy - Track blog and content performance	Ensures your visibility and budget stay optimized.
Social	- Review engagement and reach - Update your content calendar - Reply to all comments and messages - Track competitor activity	Keeps your platforms active, relevant, and engaging.
Email	- Clean your email list - Test automations and sequences - Try 1 new subject line or CTA - Track open and click rates	Improves deliverability, engagement, and ROI.

Key Metrics to Track:

Website Performance:

- Page load speed (target: under 3 seconds)

- Bounce rate (target: under 55%)

- Conversion rate (industry-dependent, typically 2-5%)

- Average session duration (target: over 2 minutes)

Traffic Generation:

- Traffic sources (aim for diversity)

- Cost per acquisition (CPA)

- Return on ad spend (ROAS)

- Organic search rankings

Social Media:

- Engagement rate (target: above 1%)

- Follower growth rate

- Response time (target: under 24 hours)

- Post reach and impressions

Email Marketing:

- Open rate (target: above 20%)

- Click-through rate (target: above 2%)

- List growth rate

- Unsubscribe rate (target: under 0.5%)

Closing Mission Brief

You've built something most small businesses never will. But don't let it stall. This checklist isn't busy work—it's how professionals stay ready for the next opportunity, the next campaign, the next move.

Chapter 9 Key Takeaways: Building Your Digital Arsenal—Core Platforms and Infrastructure

"Don't scatter your forces across the internet. Build a base, arm it well, and launch every mission from there."
—Kevin McGrew

KEY LEARNING POINTS

Your Digital Arsenal—Your War Machine

This chapter lays out the **core tech stack** and infrastructure every modern business needs to compete and win online. Think of this as **building your base before launching an attack.**

1. Your Digital Command Center: Your Website Is Home Base

- It's the only digital real estate you truly own.
- Everything—ads, content, social media—should **lead back to it.**
- Must be built for speed, clarity, conversion, and control.

Tactic: Prioritize clear messaging, fast load times, SEO best practices, and conversion pathways.

2. Establishing Supply Lines: Driving Website Traffic

- **Organic SEO** is your long-term supply chain—slow to build, but incredibly durable.
- **Paid ads** (Google, Meta, etc.) are rapid deployment tools—fast, but require constant investment.

Tactic: Use a **two-front strategy**—build SEO while running performance-based paid campaigns for immediate results.

3. Forward Operating Bases: Social Media Platforms

- ✅ Social is where your audience already lives—set up base and **engage where they are.**

- ✅ Match platform to mission:

  - B2C—Facebook, Instagram, TikTok
  - B2B—LinkedIn, YouTube

Tactic: Each platform has its own battle rhythm—build content natively for each, don't spray-and-pray.

4. Secure Communication Channels: Email and SMS

- ✅ Email—your direct line to your audience.

- ✅ SMS—rapid response for high urgency.

- ✅ Both are **mission-critical tools** for nurturing and converting leads.

Tactic: Build automated flows, segment audiences, and run campaigns with clear CTAs.

5. Local Territory Control: Own Your Market's Map

- ✅ Google Business Profile is your local war map—**control it or be invisible.**

- ✅ Local SEO—dominate your geographic niche.

Tactic: Optimize your GBP, gather reviews, and show up in the Map Pack.

Final thought: *"You can't win a war with broken gear and scattered forces. The businesses that win are the ones who treat their digital infrastructure like a military operation: planned, precise, and always battle-ready."*

The Path Forward:
A Personal Call to Action

"The time for planning is over. The time for action is now."
—Kevin McGrew

Let me speak directly to you for a moment. Yes, you—the business leader who picked up this book seeking a better way forward. I sense your determination. Your drive to succeed. Your unwillingness to accept the conventional wisdom that says smaller businesses can't compete with industry giants.

I've been where you are. When I delivered those pizza flyers door-to-door for my family's restaurant, when I tracked submarines in the Navy, when I faced off against IBM and HP for that Yahoo contract—I've felt the weight of being the underdog. But I've also experienced the thrill of victory that comes from outsmarting, rather than outspending, your competition.

Throughout this book, I've shared the **SMAC Framework** with you—**Shoot, Move, Adapt, Communicate**. But let me be crystal clear about something: this isn't a magic formula. It's not a shortcut to success or a get-rich-quick scheme. What I've given you is a battle-tested framework for strategic thinking and decisive action.

The journey ahead won't be easy. There will be setbacks. There will be moments of doubt. There will be times when the easier path seems more appealing. I know this because I've guided hundreds of businesses through this same journey. But I've also seen the transformation that happens when leaders like you fully embrace these principles.

Every week, I witness the power of these principles in action. I've seen family-owned businesses use precision targeting to carve out profitable territories in markets dominated by national chains. I've watched small manufacturers adapt their operations faster than corporate giants to seize emerging opportunities. I've guided service providers in transforming their customer relationships through strategic communication.

These aren't just isolated success stories—they represent business leaders like you who dared to think differently about competition. They're entrepreneurs who recognized that victory doesn't always go to the biggest player, but to the one who best understands and applies strategic principles.

Let me make you a promise: If you commit to implementing the principles in this book and dedicate yourself to mastering each element of the SMAC Framework, you will develop capabilities that most of your competitors don't even know exist. This isn't just about surviving in a competitive market. This is about building a business that thrives because of competition, not despite it.

Your Next Mission

Like any good commander, you need to start with clear objectives. Here's what I want you to do immediately after closing this book:

Mission 1: Launch Your Recon — Use the audit templates in Appendix A to assess your current position. Be brutally honest—know your terrain before you move.

Mission 2: Select Your First Strategic Target — Remember, you're not trying to fight on all fronts at once. Select one element from each pillar of the SMAC Framework that you can implement within the next 30 days.

Mission 3: Assemble Your Operators — You don't need a large force, but you need people who understand and believe in this approach. Share these principles with your key team members.

Mission 4: Begin Daily Market Recon — Begin monitoring your market, competitors, and operations using the frameworks I've provided. Knowledge truly is power in this battle.

I've shared a powerful strategic plan I've developed over the years to help businesses like yours outthink, outsmart, and outperform the competition. I've provided practical tips that have proven successful in helping companies defeat larger rivals. Now, it's time for you to take these tools and put them into action with confidence.

The battlefield is waiting. Your competitors are out there—probably doing what they've always done, probably believing their size or resources guarantee success. But you and I know differently. We know that victory goes to the strategic thinker, the agile mover, the precise shooter, and the clear communicator.

You're not just an entrepreneur anymore. You're a battlefield commander—strategic, decisive, and dangerous to your competition. The tools are in your hands. The framework is clear. The path forward is marked.

Will it be challenging? Absolutely. Will it require dedication and persistence? Without question. But I promise you this: If you commit to this journey, if you implement these principles with discipline and determination, you will develop capabilities that will serve you not just today, but for years to come.

The future belongs to those who move first, adapt fast, and lead without hesitation. Through the SMAC Framework, you now have the strategic foundation to be among them.

You've read the manual. Now enter the field. This is your rally point.

Move out, and secure your victory.

–Kevin McGrew

> *"You've read the manual. Now enter the field. This is your rally point."*
> Join the War Room and stay in formation with other SMAC Operators.

Join Us In The War Room

Step into the War Room Now

About the Author

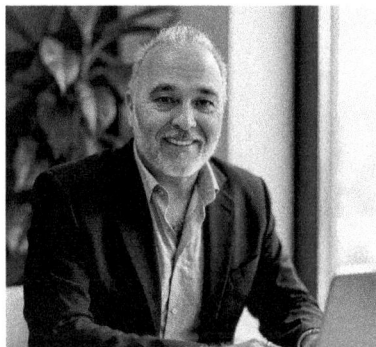

Kevin McGrew's journey from Navy sailor to marketing innovator is one of strategy, adaptability, and a relentless drive to help underdogs win.

Serving aboard the USS Long Beach, CGN-9, Kevin learned that winning battles depends on precision and agility, lessons he carried into his career.

After leading companies across industries—scaling franchises, managing IT systems, and launching startups—he saw a recurring problem: smaller businesses struggled not due to lack of value but lack of strategy.

This realization led Kevin to found Everzocial, a digital marketing agency dedicated to helping small and mid-sized businesses thrive against larger competitors. Under his leadership, Everzocial has become a beacon of innovation, leveraging strategies like the SMAC Framework (Shoot, Move, Adapt, Communicate) to help clients turn limited resources into competitive advantages.

Known for his battle-tested insights and straight-talking style, Kevin is also a mentor, thought leader, and lifelong learner whose passion for helping others fuels his work. Through *the SMAC Framework*, Kevin provides businesses with the tools to outthink, outmaneuver, and outperform the competition.

Ready to Join the Fight?

If this book spoke to you, don't go to war alone. Join the *Marketing Warfare HQ* community and connect with fellow entrepreneurs and underdog marketers who are fighting smarter every day.

- Enlist: MarketingWarfareHQ.com
- LinkedIn: Kevin McGrew
- Instagram: @iamkevin
- X (Twitter): @smacmarketer
- Facebook: Kevin McGrew, Author
- ▶ YouTube: youtube.com/@smacmarketer

THE USS LONG BEACH CGN-9: A LEGACY OF INNOVATION AND STRENGTH

The USS Long Beach wasn't just a warship—it was a leap forward in naval innovation, a symbol of strategic dominance during the Cold War.

Launched in 1961 and serving as the world's first nuclear-powered guided missile cruiser, the Long Beach was a marvel of its time. But by the mid-1980s, during my tenure aboard from 1985 to 1988, the ship had evolved into an even more formidable presence on the seas.

> *"The Long Beach wasn't just a ship—it was a masterclass in how vision, technology, and strategy can come together to redefine what's possible."*

A Visionary Innovation: The First Phased-Array Radar System

The USS Long Beach was ahead of its time, introducing phased-array radar—a breakthrough that changed naval warfare forever. Its radar system, an early version of what would become the Aegis Combat System, could track and engage multiple targets at once. This game-changing tech set a new standard for ship defense and still powers modern naval fleets around the world today.

Power and Precision: The Ship's Advanced Capabilities

The Long Beach was no ordinary cruiser. Powered by two nuclear reactors, it had an unlimited range and could cruise at speeds exceeding 30 knots. The ship's arsenal was a testament to innovation:

- BGM-109 Tomahawk Cruise Missiles: Capable of striking deep into enemy territory with pinpoint accuracy, these missiles represented the cutting edge of strategic deterrence.

- Harpoon Anti-Ship Missiles: These versatile weapons gave the ship unparalleled reach against surface targets.

- Standard SM-2ER Missiles: These provided long-range air defense, capable of neutralizing incoming threats before they reached the fleet.

- Phalanx CIWS Systems: Known as the last line of defense, these rapid-firing Gatling guns intercepted enemy missiles and aircraft with devastating speed.

Cold War Mission: A Show of Strength and Resolve

During the 1980s, the Long Beach was central to America's naval strategy in the Cold War. Under President Reagan's administration, the ship symbolized U.S. military might and technological superiority. As tensions with the Soviet Union escalated, the Long Beach was frequently deployed to demonstrate American resolve in critical regions.

From 1987 to 1988, the ship played a pivotal role in the Persian Gulf during Operation Nimble Archer, a high-profile response to Iranian aggression. Operating in the Western Pacific, Indian Ocean, and the volatile Persian Gulf, the Long Beach provided anti-aircraft coverage, conducted Tomahawk cruise missile tests, and supported strategic naval operations that underscored America's presence in critical international waters.

"Strike Hard, Strike Home"

The ship's motto, "Strike Hard, Strike Home," was not just a rallying cry—it was a reflection of its mission and capabilities. Whether launching missiles in precision drills or navigating the narrow, tense waters of the Gulf, the Long Beach embodied decisive action, resilience, and innovation.

A Personal Legacy

Serving aboard the USS Long Beach during its most influential years left an indelible mark on me. The lessons I learned—precision in planning, adaptability in execution, and clarity in communication—shaped my approach to marketing and strategy. Much like the Long Beach, businesses today must leverage innovation and agility to navigate complex, competitive landscapes.

The USS Long Beach CGN-9 wasn't just a ship; it was a masterclass in

how vision, technology, and strategy can come together to redefine what's possible. Its legacy endures, not only in the annals of naval history but also in the lessons it offers to those willing to embrace ingenuity and adaptability in their own battles. *Fair winds and following seas, wherever your mission takes you.*

The SMAC Marketer's Creed

I am a SMAC Marketer.
I fight for the overlooked, the underestimated, the underdog.
I am trained in strategy, forged in adversity, and committed to execution.

I will Shoot with precision—never wasting a word, a click, or a dollar.
I will Move with purpose—staying agile, adapting fast, and never standing still.
I will Adapt to win—reading the terrain, shifting tactics, outsmarting the giants.
I will Communicate with clarity—cutting through noise, commanding attention, and driving action.

I do not flinch at competition.
I do not retreat in the face of complexity.
I do not follow trends—I study them, weaponize them, and outmaneuver them.

My tools are data and instinct.
My weapon is the SMAC Framework.
My battlefield is wherever attention is earned and trust is won.

I lead by example.
I market with honor.
I build brands that last, not hype that fades.
In every campaign, I will remain focused, relentless, and dangerous.
I will lift my fellow strategists.
I will sharpen my skill daily.
I will leave no insight unused, no audience unfelt, no message unclear.

I am not a service provider.
I am not a vendor.
I am a SMAC Marketer.
A strategist.
A force.

Shoot. Move. Adapt. Communicate.
Victory Favors the Strategic.
SMAC ON. #SMACMarketer

APPENDIX A: DIGITAL MARKETING ARSENAL AUDIT TEMPLATES

Understanding your strengths, coupled with comprehensive evaluations of your processes, is crucial for achieving military success. During my tenure on one of the US Navy's most advanced warships, we performed consistent readiness assessments—not solely to pinpoint vulnerabilities but also to guarantee our capability to respond swiftly to any situation. This principle is equally vital for your digital marketing operations.

Throughout my journey as an entrepreneur and owner of a marketing agency, I've witnessed firsthand how conducting regular audits can revitalize struggling businesses, turning them into efficient powerhouses.

One standout example is a regional manufacturing client that was exhausting its marketing budget without seeing results. By utilizing targeted audit templates, they pinpointed significant weaknesses in their digital infrastructure and strategically reallocated their resources. Just six months later, they were not only competing but were also surpassing rivals that were three times their size.

These audit templates are your tactical assessment tools. They're designed to help you:

- Evaluate your current digital marketing capabilities

- Identify strategic weaknesses before they become vulnerabilities

- Prioritize improvements based on impact and urgency

- Track progress over time

- Maintain operational readiness

Think of these templates as your combat readiness reports. Just as military commanders need accurate assessments of their forces' capabilities, you need clear insights into your digital marketing arsenal. These aren't just checklists—they're strategic tools that will help you maintain battlefield superiority in an increasingly competitive digital landscape.

How to use these templates:

1. Regular Assessment Schedule: Conduct comprehensive audits quarterly, with monthly check-ins on critical metrics. This cadence allows you to identify trends and address issues before they become critical.

2. Scoring System: Each template uses a consistent scoring system that helps you:

   - Quantify your current capabilities

   - Track improvements over time

   - Compare performance across different areas

   - Prioritize resource allocation

3. Action Planning: Every section includes:

   - Priority markers for urgent issues

   - Improvement recommendations

   - Resource allocation guidance

   - Implementation timelines

Remember, in both military operations and marketing strategies, having high-quality intelligence and a truthful evaluation of your capabilities can outweigh sheer force. Utilize these templates as your strategic planning tools; they will guide you in determining the most effective allocation of resources for optimal results.

A note on adaptability: These templates are comprehensive, but they're also adaptable. Just as military units modify their tactics based on terrain and mission parameters, you should adjust these assessments based on your specific industry and objectives. The key is maintaining the rigorous evaluation standard while adapting the specific metrics to your battlefield conditions.

Now, let's examine your digital marketing arsenal with the precision of a military inspection and the strategic insight of a seasoned commander. Your audit begins here.

DIGITAL MARKETING ARSENAL AUDIT TEMPLATES

Introduction: Just as military commanders conduct regular readiness assessments, these audit templates will help you evaluate the strength of your digital marketing arsenal. Each template includes:

- Capability assessment criteria

- Performance metrics

- Strategic importance ratings

- Action priority levels

- Improvement recommendations

Template 1: COMMAND CENTER (WEBSITE) AUDIT

Strategic Objective: Assess the strength and effectiveness of your primary base of operations

Section A: Technical Readiness Score each item:

0 (Not Present) | 1 (Needs Improvement) | 2 (Satisfactory) | 3 (Excellent)

Security & Infrastructure:
___ SSL Certificate active
___ Mobile responsiveness
___ Page load speed (under 3 seconds)
___ Backup system in place
___ Website uptime monitoring

Technical SEO:
___ XML sitemap
___ Robots.txt configured
___ Meta titles and descriptions
___ Header tag hierarchy
___ Image optimization

Analytics & Tracking:
___ Google Analytics installed
___ Goal tracking configured
___ Event tracking active
___ Form tracking setup
___ Search console integration

Section B: Content Effectiveness Score each item:

0 (Missing) | 1 (Basic) | 2 (Good) | 3 (Outstanding)

Core Content:
___ Homepage messaging
___ About page completeness
___ Service/Product pages
___ Contact information
___ Call-to-action clarity

Content Strategy:
___ Blog/News section
___ Case studies/Portfolio
___ Testimonials/Reviews
___ Resource section
___ FAQ page

Section C: Conversion Optimization
___ Lead capture forms
___ Contact forms
___ Email signup forms
___ Chat functionality
___ Appointment booking system

Total Score: _____ /75

Readiness Level: 65-75
Elite Force 50-64
Battle Ready 35-49
Scores Below 35: Critical Improvement Needed

Template 2: SUPPLY LINES (TRAFFIC) AUDIT

Strategic Objective: Evaluate effectiveness of traffic generation strategies

Section A: Organic Traffic Assessment

Current Monthly Organic Traffic: _____

Year-over-Year Growth: _____%

SEO Performance:

___ Keyword rankings

___ Organic visibility

___ Content performance

___ Backlink profile

___ Local search presence

Section B: Paid Traffic Assessment

Current Monthly Paid Traffic: _____

Cost Per Acquisition: $_____

Campaign Performance:

___ Search ads

___ Display ads

___ Social ads

___ Remarketing

___ Video ads

Template 3: SOCIAL MEDIA (FORWARD OPERATING BASES) AUDIT

Strategic Objective: Evaluate effectiveness of social media outposts and engagement capabilities

Section A: Platform Presence Assessment

Score each active platform: 0 (Inactive) | 1 (Basic) | 2 (Active) | 3 (Optimized)

Section A: Organic Traffic Assessment	Section B: Paid Traffic Assessment
Current Monthly Organic Traffic: _____	Current Monthly Paid Traffic: _____
Year-over-Year Growth: _____%	Cost Per Acquisition: $_____
SEO Performance:	**Campaign Performance:**
___ Keyword rankings	___ Search ads
___ Organic visibility	___ Display ads
___ Content performance	___ Social ads
___ Backlink profile	___ Remarketing
___ Local search presence	___ Video ads

Facebook:	Instagram:	LinkedIn (B2B):
___ Profile completeness	___ Visual branding	___ Company page optimization
___ Posting frequency	___ Story utilization	___ Content relevance
___ Engagement rate	___ Reels implementation	___ Professional engagement
___ Response time	___ Hashtag strategy	___ Employee advocacy
___ Community management	___ Engagement quality	___ Lead generation

Section B: Content Strategy Assessment

Score each item: 0 (None) | 1 (Basic) | 2 (Good) | 3 (Excellent)

Content Planning:	Engagement Metrics:
___ Editorial calendar	___ Follower growth rate
___ Content mix	___ Engagement per post
___ Brand voice consistency	___ Share/Save rate
___ Visual consistency	___ Comment quality
___ Value proposition clarity	___ Click-through rate

Template 4: COMMUNICATION INFRA-STRUCTURE AUDIT

Strategic Objective: Assess effectiveness of direct communication channels

Section A: Email Marketing Assessment

List Size: _____

Average Open Rate: ____%

Average Click Rate: ____%

Platform Optimization:

___ Automation workflows

___ List segmentation

___ Template design

___ Mobile optimization

___ Deliverability rate

Campaign Effectiveness:

___ Welcome sequence

___ Nurture campaigns

___ Promotional emails

___ Re-engagement campaigns

___ Retention communications

Section B: SMS Marketing Assessment

List Size: _____

Average Response Rate: ____%

Opt-out Rate: ____%

Implementation:

___ Compliance measures

___ Integration with email

___ Automated responses

___ Segmentation strategy

___ Performance tracking

Template 5: LOCAL TERRITORY CONTROL AUDIT

Strategic Objective: Evaluate local search presence and reputation management

Section A: Email Marketing Assessment

List Size: _____

Average Open Rate: ____%

Average Click Rate: ____%

Platform Optimization:

___ Automation workflows

___ List segmentation

___ Template design

___ Mobile optimization

___ Deliverability rate

Campaign Effectiveness:

___ Welcome sequence

___ Nurture campaigns

___ Promotional emails

___ Re-engagement campaigns

___ Retention communications

Section B: SMS Marketing Assessment

List Size: _____

Average Response Rate: ____%

Opt-out Rate: ____%

Implementation:

___ Compliance measures

___ Integration with email

___ Automated responses

___ Segmentation strategy

___ Performance tracking

Section A: Google Business Profile Assessment

Score each item: 0 (Not Done) | 1 (Basic) | 2 (Good) | 3 (Excellent)

Profile Optimization:

___ Business information accuracy

___ Photo quality and quantity

___ Post frequency

___ Q&A management

___ Category selection

Review Management:

___ Total review count

___ Average rating

___ Response rate

___ Response quality

___ Review generation system

Section B: Local Search Presence

Current Map Pack Position: _____

Number of Local Keywords Ranking: _____

Local SEO:

___ Citation consistency

___ Local content

___ Local backlinks

___ Schema markup

___ Local landing pages

COMPREHENSIVE SCORING MATRIX

Total all section scores to determine overall digital marketing readiness:

Elite Force (90%+):

- Dominant market position
- Highly effective systems
- Regular optimization
- Clear competitive advantage

Battle Ready (75-89%):

- Strong market presence
- Effective core systems
- Regular maintenance
- Competitive positioning

Needs Reinforcement (60-74%):

- Basic market presence
- Core systems in place
- Irregular maintenance
- Limited competitive edge

Critical Improvement Needed (Below 60%):

- Weak market presence
- Incomplete systems
- Minimal maintenance
- Competitive disadvantage

ACTION PRIORITY MATRIX

Score each improvement opportunity: Impact (1-5) × Urgency (1-5) = Priority Score

Priority Levels:

20-25: Immediate Action Required

15-19: High Priority

10-14: Medium Priority

5-9: Low Priority

Glossary of 100+ Marketing Warfare Terms

A

Adaptive Combat Evolution (ACE):

Definition: The continuous process of improving marketing strategies through real-time learning and adaptation to market conditions.

Example: Constantly refining social media content strategy based on engagement analytics.

Adaptive Intelligence:

Definition: The ability to learn from market feedback and modify marketing strategies in real time based on performance data and changing conditions.

Example: Using A/B testing results to continuously refine email marketing campaigns.

Advocate Activation Protocol:

Definition: Systematic approach to identifying, engaging, and empowering loyal customers to become brand ambassadors.

Example: Converting satisfied customers into active referral sources through structured engagement programs.

Ammunition Conservation:

Definition: The strategic allocation and management of marketing resources to maximize impact while minimizing waste.

Example: Carefully allocating advertising budget across the highest-performing channels rather than spreading it thinly across all platforms.

Army of Advocates:

Definition: A network of loyal customers and brand supporters who actively promote and defend the brand through word-of-mouth and social proof.

Example: Customers who consistently share positive experiences on social media and refer new clients.

Asymmetric Marketing:

Definition: Marketing strategies that leverage a smaller company's unique advantages to compete effectively against larger competitors.

Example: A local business using personalized service and community connections to compete with national chains.

B

Battle Damage Assessment (BDA):

Definition: The process of evaluating marketing campaign effectiveness through data analysis and performance metrics to determine success and areas for improvement.

Example: Analyzing email campaign metrics like open rates, click-through rates, and conversion data to assess campaign impact.

Battle Rhythm:

Definition: The coordinated timing and sequencing of marketing activities to maintain a consistent market presence and impact.

Example: Synchronized content publishing, email campaigns, and social media posting schedules.

Battlefield Intelligence:

Definition: Comprehensive market research and competitive analysis that provides strategic insights for decision-making.

Example: Analyzing competitor strategies, customer behavior patterns, and market trends to inform marketing decisions.

Battlefield Momentum:

Definition: The accumulated advantage gained through consistent successful marketing actions that create forward movement in market share and brand recognition.

Example: Building upon viral content success to launch larger marketing initiatives.

Battlefield Momentum Indicators:

Definition: Metrics that measure the rate and direction of market share changes and brand growth over time.

Example: Tracking week-over-week increases in website traffic, social media followers, and conversion rates.

Battlefield Surveillance System:

Definition: Comprehensive monitoring of market activities, competitor movements, and customer behavior patterns.

Example: Using social listening tools and analytics to track industry trends and competitive actions.

Brand Fortification:

Definition: Strategic actions taken to strengthen brand identity and protect market position against competitive threats.

Example: Building strong customer relationships through loyalty programs and exceptional service.

C

Combat Evolution:

Definition: The continuous process of improving and adapting marketing strategies based on market intelligence and performance data.

Example: A company evolving its social media strategy based on engagement metrics and audience feedback.

Combat Evolution Cycle:

Definition: The continuous process of learning, adapting, and improving marketing strategies based on performance data.

Example: Regular review and refinement of marketing tactics based on campaign results.

Combat Information Center (CIC):

Definition: Central hub for monitoring, analyzing, and coordinating all marketing activities and campaign performance.

Example: Marketing department's central command post where all campaign metrics and market data are monitored.

Combat Intelligence Dashboard:

Definition: A centralized system for monitoring and analyzing key marketing metrics, competitor activities, and market trends in real time.

Example: Digital dashboard tracking social media engagement, website traffic, and conversion rates simultaneously.

Combat Logistics:

Definition: The management and coordination of marketing resources, tools, and capabilities to support ongoing campaigns.

Example: Coordinating content creation, distribution, and promotion across multiple channels.

Combat Readiness Assessment:

Definition: Regular evaluation of marketing capabilities, resources, and systems to ensure operational effectiveness.

Example: Monthly audit of marketing tools, team skills, and campaign performance metrics.

Combat Zone:

Definition: The specific market or industry segment where a business competes, including all relevant competitors, customers, and environmental factors.

Example: A defined market space where businesses compete for customer attention and sales.

Command & Control:

Definition: The centralized management and coordination of marketing efforts across multiple channels and campaigns to ensure consistent messaging and optimal results.

Example: Coordinating all marketing activities through a central strategy team.

Command & Control Infrastructure:

Definition: The technological and organizational systems that enable coordinated marketing operations across multiple channels.

Example: Marketing automation platforms, CRM systems, and team communication tools.

Command Center:

Definition: The central hub of marketing operations, typically a company's website, where all marketing activities are coordinated and controlled.

Example: A company's website serves as the primary platform for customer engagement and conversion.

Cross-Channel Communication Strategy:

Definition: A coordinated approach to delivering consistent messaging across multiple marketing platforms and touchpoints.

Example: Maintaining brand voice consistency across website, social media, email, and advertising campaigns.

D

Digital Arsenal:

Definition: The complete set of digital marketing tools, platforms, and technologies a business uses to compete in the marketplace.

Example: Suite of marketing tools including CRM, social media management, email marketing, and analytics platforms.

Digital Perimeter Defense:

Definition: Strategies and systems implemented to protect and maintain a brand's online reputation and market position.

Example: Monitoring and responding to online reviews and social media mentions.

Digital Reconnaissance:

Definition: The systematic gathering of online market intelligence through various digital channels and tools.

Example: Using social listening tools and web analytics to track competitor activities and customer behavior.

Digital Supply Chain:

Definition: The complete system of tools, platforms, and processes that deliver content and messages to target audiences.

Example: Content management systems, distribution networks, and delivery platforms working in coordination.

Digital Terrain Analysis:

Definition: Assessment of the online landscape, including competitor presence, customer behavior patterns, and channel effectiveness.

Example: Mapping customer journey touchpoints across different digital platforms.

Digital Territory Control:

Definition: The establishment and maintenance of a strong online presence in specific digital channels or market segments.

Example: Dominating local search results for specific industry keywords.

E

Engagement Battle Space:

Definition: The various channels and platforms where brands compete for customer attention and interaction.

Example: Social media platforms, email inboxes, and content consumption environments.

Engagement Superiority:

Definition: Achieving higher levels of meaningful customer interaction and engagement compared to competitors.

Example: Maintaining higher social media engagement rates and customer response levels.

Engagement Velocity:

Definition: The speed and frequency at which a brand's content and messaging generate meaningful audience interaction.

Example: Measuring the rate of social media responses and comment activity on posts.

F

FAW (Find Another Way):

Definition: A core mindset emphasizing creative problem-solving and alternative approaches when faced with obstacles or limited resources.

Example: Developing creative solutions when traditional marketing approaches are too costly or ineffective.

Field Intelligence Network:

Definition: A system of information gathering from various market sources, including customers, employees, and industry contacts.

Example: Customer feedback surveys, sales team reports, and industry forum monitoring.

First Mover Advantage Protocol:

Definition: Strategic framework for identifying and capitalizing on new market opportunities before competitors.

Example: Being first to market with innovative content formats or marketing approaches.

Force Multiplication:

Definition: Strategies or tactics that amplify marketing impact beyond the direct investment of resources.

Example: Using user-generated content to expand reach without increasing marketing spend.

Force Multiplier Content:

Definition: Marketing content that generates exponential impact through sharing and viral effects.

Example: Highly shareable infographics or videos that spread organically through social networks.

Force Protection Measures:

Definition: Strategies and systems implemented to protect brand reputation and market position from competitive threats.

Example: Proactive reputation management and crisis communication plans.

Forward Operating Bases:

Definition: Secondary marketing platforms and channels that extend a brand's reach beyond its primary website.

Example: Social media profiles, marketplace listings, and industry directory presence.

Forward Scout Analytics:

Definition: Predictive analysis tools and methods used to identify emerging market opportunities and threats.

Example: Using trend analysis and predictive modeling to forecast market changes.

Future Combat Operations:

Definition: Strategic planning and preparation for emerging marketing technologies and trends to maintain competitive advantage.

Example: Developing capabilities in AI marketing automation and virtual reality customer experiences.

G

Ground Force Operations:

Definition: Direct, personal marketing activities that involve face-to-face interaction with customers or prospects.

Example: Trade show presentations, local community events, and in-store promotions.

Guerrilla Intelligence Network:

Definition: Informal channels and sources for gathering market insights and competitive intelligence.

Example: Customer feedback, industry connections, and front-line employee observations.

Guerrilla Tactics:

Definition: Unconventional, low-cost marketing approaches that leverage creativity and surprise to achieve maximum impact with minimal resources.

Example: Creating viral social media content through clever, timely responses to current events.

H

High-Ground Strategy:

Definition: Positioning a brand in a superior market position that is difficult for competitors to challenge.

Example: Establishing unique expertise or specialized service offerings in a niche market.

High-Value Targets:

Definition: Ideal customers or market segments that offer the greatest potential return on marketing investment.

Example: Identifying and focusing on customer segments with the highest lifetime value potential.

I

Impact Assessment Matrix:

Definition: A structured framework for evaluating the effectiveness and ROI of marketing initiatives across multiple metrics.

Example: Scoring system that measures campaign success across engagement, conversion, and revenue metrics.

Intelligence Amplification Network:

Definition: System for maximizing the value of market intelligence through collaborative analysis and sharing.

Example: Cross-departmental meetings to share customer insights and market observations.

Intelligence Fusion Center (IFC):

Definition: A centralized system for collecting, analyzing, and distributing market intelligence across the organization.

Example: Weekly intelligence briefings combining data from multiple sources and departments.

Intelligence-Gathering Systems (IGS):

Definition: Tools and processes used to collect, analyze, and utilize market data and customer insights for strategic decision-making.

Example: Using analytics platforms, social listening tools, and customer feedback systems.

Intelligence Verification Protocol:

Definition: Process for validating and confirming market intelligence before using it in strategic decisions.

Example: Cross-referencing multiple data sources to confirm market trends before acting.

L

Local Theater Operations:

Definition: Marketing activities focused on specific geographic or demographic market segments.

Example: Targeted campaigns designed for particular neighborhoods or community groups.

M

Market Intelligence Fusion:

Definition: Process of combining multiple sources of market data to create comprehensive insights.

Example: Integrating customer feedback, sales data, and market research into unified intelligence.

Market Intelligence Network:

Definition: Interconnected system of tools, sources, and processes for gathering and analyzing market information.

Example: Combination of social listening tools, analytics platforms, and customer feedback systems.

Market Maneuver Warfare:

Definition: Strategic approach focusing on rapid, coordinated actions to outmaneuver competitors and capture market opportunities.

Example: Quick product launches or promotional campaigns in response to market gaps.

Market Penetration Strategy:

Definition: Tactical approaches to entering and establishing presence in new market segments or territories.

Example: Using targeted content marketing to build authority in a new industry vertical.

Market Position Defense Grid:

Definition: Structured approach to protecting established market positions against various competitive threats.

Example: Multi-layered strategy combining customer retention, brand loyalty, and competitive differentiation.

Market Position Fortification:

Definition: Strategies implemented to strengthen and defend a brand's established market position against competitive threats.

Example: Building strong customer loyalty programs and creating unique value propositions.

Market Position Radar:

Definition: System for monitoring and tracking changes in market position relative to competitors.

Example: Regular assessment of brand awareness, market share, and competitive standing.

Marketing Special Forces:

Definition: Highly trained marketing teams capable of executing complex, precision-targeted campaigns and responding rapidly to market opportunities.

Example: Specialized teams trained in rapid response and high-impact campaign execution.

Message Clarity:

Definition: The ability to communicate value propositions and brand messages in a clear, compelling, and consistent manner.

Example: Developing simple, memorable taglines that effectively communicate unique selling points.

O

Operational Agility:

Definition: The capability to quickly adjust marketing operations and tactics in response to market feedback or opportunities.

Example: Rapidly modifying campaign messaging based on real-time performance data.

Operational Resilience:

Definition: The ability to maintain marketing effectiveness despite disruptions or resource constraints.

Example: Maintaining campaign performance during budget cuts or market downturns.

Operational Security (OPSEC):

Definition: Practices and procedures to protect sensitive marketing strategies and competitive advantages from competitors.

Example: Maintaining confidentiality of new product development and campaign planning.

Operational Synchronization:

Definition: Coordination of various marketing activities to achieve maximum combined impact.

Example: Aligning social media, email, and advertising campaigns for product launches.

Operational Tempo:

Definition: The pace and rhythm at which marketing activities are executed to maintain a consistent market presence.

Example: Regular content publishing schedule and campaign launch frequency.

P

Precision Content Deployment:

Definition: Strategic distribution of content to specific audience segments at optimal times.

Example: Scheduling social media posts based on audience activity patterns.

Precision Impact Assessment:

Definition: Detailed analysis of marketing campaign effectiveness across multiple metrics and dimensions.

Example: Measuring campaign ROI across different customer segments and channels.

Precision Impact Zones:

Definition: Specific areas or segments where marketing efforts can achieve maximum effect.

Example: High-value customer segments or particularly responsive market niches.

Precision Response Matrix:

Definition: Framework for determining appropriate responses to various market situations or competitor actions.

Example: Predetermined strategies for responding to competitor price changes or promotional activities.

Precision Strike Planning:

Definition: The detailed preparation and coordination of targeted marketing campaigns designed for maximum impact.

Example: Developing highly targeted email sequences for specific customer segments.

Precision Targeting:

Definition: The practice of identifying and engaging specific audience segments with highly relevant messaging and offers.

Example: Creating personalized email campaigns based on customer behavior and preferences.

Precision Targeting Matrix:

Definition: Framework for identifying and prioritizing high-value target audiences based on multiple criteria.

Example: Scoring system combining demographic, behavioral, and value-based factors.

Q

Quick Response Force (QRF):

Definition: A dedicated team or system capable of responding rapidly to market opportunities or challenges.

Example: Social media team ready to engage with trending topics relevant to the brand.

Quick Strike Capability:

Definition: The ability to rapidly deploy marketing initiatives in response to opportunities or threats.

Example: Launching targeted social media campaigns within hours of market developments.

R

Rapid Deployment Content:

Definition: Pre-prepared marketing content that can be quickly modified and deployed in response to market opportunities.

Example: Template-based social media posts that can be customized for trending topics.

Rapid Response Artillery:

Definition: Quick-deployment marketing assets and campaigns ready for immediate use.

Example: Pre-prepared social media templates and emergency response content.

Rapid Response Protocols:

Definition: Predetermined procedures for quickly addressing market changes, opportunities, or challenges.

Example: Having a crisis communication plan ready for immediate deployment.

Resource Audit & Optimization:

Definition: The systematic evaluation and improvement of marketing assets, tools, and capabilities to maximize effectiveness.

Example: Analyzing marketing technology stack efficiency and eliminating redundant tools.

Resource Concentration:

Definition: Strategic focusing of marketing resources on high-priority targets or opportunities.

Example: Allocating the majority of the budget to the highest-performing channels or campaigns.

Resource Deployment Matrix:

Definition: A strategic framework for allocating marketing resources across various channels and initiatives based on potential impact.

Example: Budget allocation model that prioritizes the highest-performing marketing channels.

S

SMAC Framework:

Definition: A comprehensive marketing strategy framework consisting of four key elements: Shoot (precision targeting), Move (tactical agility), Adapt (combat evolution), and Communicate (command & control).

Example: Implementing all four elements to create a coordinated marketing approach.

SMAC Marketer

Definition: A SMAC Marketer is a modern-day strategist trained to outthink, outmaneuver, and out-communicate bigger competitors—using precision, agility, adaptability, and clarity.

Example: Long Live the SMAC Marketer.

Strategic Asset Deployment (SAD):

Definition: Systematic allocation of marketing resources and capabilities for maximum strategic advantage.

Example: Distributing content and campaign resources across the highest-impact channels.

Strategic Command Protocol:

Definition: Framework for making and implementing strategic marketing decisions efficiently.

Example: Decision-making hierarchy and approval processes for marketing initiatives.

Strategic Communication Protocol:

Definition: Standardized procedures for ensuring consistent and effective communication across all marketing channels.

Example: Guidelines for maintaining brand voice and messaging across different platforms.

Strategic Depth:

Definition: The extent of backup plans, alternative strategies, and reserve resources available for marketing operations.

Example: Having multiple campaign variations ready for different market scenarios.

Strategic Evolution Framework:

Definition: A structured approach to continuously improving and adapting marketing strategies based on performance data and market changes.

Example: Regular review and update cycles for marketing tactics based on measured results.

Strategic Pivot Points:

Definition: Key moments or triggers that signal the need for significant changes in marketing strategy or tactics.

Example: Shifting from traditional advertising to digital channels based on changing consumer behavior.

Strategic Reserve:

Definition: Marketing resources and capabilities held in reserve for opportunistic deployment or emergency response.

Example: Emergency marketing budget or pre-prepared crisis communication materials.

Strategic Reserve Assets:

Definition: Marketing resources and capabilities held in reserve for opportunistic deployment or crisis response.

Example: Emergency marketing budget or backup content libraries.

Supply Lines:

Definition: The channels and methods used to generate consistent traffic and leads for a business.

Example: SEO, paid advertising, and referral partnerships that drive website visitors.

T

Tactical Agility:

Definition: The ability to quickly adjust marketing strategies and tactics in response to market changes or opportunities.

Example: Rapidly shifting marketing messages during sudden market changes.

Tactical Deployment:

Definition: The execution of specific marketing initiatives or campaigns according to strategic objectives.

Example: Launching a coordinated social media campaign across multiple platforms.

Tactical Engagement Matrix:

Definition: Framework for determining appropriate engagement strategies for different audience segments.

Example: Customized communication approaches for different customer types.

Tactical Evolution Framework:

Definition: System for continuously improving and adapting marketing tactics based on performance data and market feedback.

Example: Regular review and optimization cycle for marketing campaigns and strategies.

Tactical Flexibility:

Definition: The ability to quickly modify marketing tactics based on changing conditions or feedback.

Example: Adjusting campaign messaging based on real-time performance data.

Tactical Resource Matrix:

Definition: System for allocating marketing resources based on strategic priorities and opportunities.

Example: Budget and resource allocation framework for different marketing channels.

Tactical Response Grid:

Definition: A predetermined set of responses to common market situations or competitor actions.

Example: Decision matrix for responding to competitor price changes or promotional activities.

Tactical Response Time:

Definition: The speed at which an organization can implement marketing responses to market changes or opportunities.

Example: Time taken to launch a counter-campaign in response to competitor actions.

Target Acquisition Protocol:

Definition: Systematic process for identifying and qualifying potential high-value customers or market segments.

Example: Lead scoring system based on behavioral and demographic data.

Territory Defense:

Definition: Strategies and tactics used to maintain market share and competitive advantage in established markets.

Example: Implementing customer retention programs and loyalty initiatives.

Territory Expansion Protocol:

Definition: Systematic approach for entering and establishing presence in new markets or segments.

Example: Phased rollout plan for entering new geographic markets or customer segments.

V

Victory Conditions:

Definition: Clearly defined objectives and metrics that constitute success for marketing campaigns or strategic initiatives.

Example: Specific KPIs for market share, revenue growth, or customer acquisition targets.

Victory Maintenance:

Definition: The ongoing effort to sustain and build upon marketing successes through continuous improvement and adaptation.

Example: Regular optimization of successful campaigns and expansion into related market segments.

Victory Metrics:

Definition: Key performance indicators that define success in marketing campaigns and strategic initiatives.

Example: Specific targets for market share growth, customer acquisition, and revenue increase.

Victory Path Mapping:

Definition: Strategic planning process that outlines steps and milestones toward marketing objectives.

Example: Detailed roadmap showing key achievements needed for market leadership.

Victory Reinforcement Protocol:

Definition: Systems and processes for maintaining and building upon marketing successes.

Example: Programs to extend and expand successful campaign results.

Victory Sustainability Index:

Definition: Measure of an organization's ability to maintain and build upon marketing successes over time.

Example: Long-term customer retention rates and market share stability metrics.

W

War Room Analytics:

Definition: The centralized monitoring and analysis of marketing performance metrics to inform strategic decisions.

Example: Dashboard monitoring of key performance indicators across all marketing channels.

Warfare Analytics:

Definition: Comprehensive analysis of competitive market dynamics and performance metrics to inform strategic decisions.

Example: Tracking competitor activities, market share changes, and customer behavior patterns.

Warfare Analytics Dashboard:

Definition: Comprehensive system for monitoring and analyzing competitive market dynamics and campaign performance.

Example: Real-time tracking of market share, competitor activities, and campaign metrics.

Warfare Intelligence Cycle:

Definition: The continuous process of collecting, analyzing, and acting on market intelligence.

Example: Regular cycle of market research, competitor analysis, and strategy adjustment.

Weapons of Mass Attraction:

Definition: High-impact marketing assets or campaigns that generate significant audience engagement and response. Also known as "Lead Magnets".

Example: Viral content pieces or highly successful lead magnets that consistently drive results.

Z

Zero-Hour Response:

Definition: Immediate tactical adjustments made in response to sudden market changes or opportunities.

Example: Real-time social media engagement during trending events relevant to the brand.

Zone Defense Marketing:

Definition: Strategy of focusing marketing efforts on defending and dominating specific market segments or territories.

Example: Concentrating resources on maintaining leadership in specific geographic or demographic segments.

Zone of Influence:

Definition: The geographic, demographic, or psychographic areas where a brand maintains strong market presence and customer loyalty.

Example: Core customer segments or geographic regions where the brand holds a dominant market share.

Final Orders

Your mission doesn't end here.
You've read the Battle Plan.
You've absorbed the strategy.

Now it's time to enter the war room.
The marketing battlefield is constantly shifting.
New threats. New tactics. New opportunities.
And the most dangerous place you can be—is alone.

That's why we built **Marketing Warfare HQ.**

It's more than a community.
It's a command center.
A live briefing room.
A place for Strategists like you to train, share intelligence, and execute with precision.

Inside, you'll get:

- Live Tactical Calls & Strategy Breakdowns
- Case Studies from Fellow SMAC Marketers
- Exclusive Content & Playbooks
- Private War Rooms by Industry & Specialty
- Early Intel on Tools, Trends & Tactics
- Accountability. Brotherhood. Victory.

Whether you're a solo commando or leading a squad—this is your next move.

Scan the QR Code or visit marketingwarfarehq.com

Join us in the War Room. Become a SMAC Marketer.

Join Us In The War Room

Shoot. Move. Adapt. Communicate.

Victory Favors the Strategic.

SMAC ON.

#SMACMarketer | #MarketingWarfare | #BuiltToSMAC

THE BATTLE CRY: This Isn't Just a Book. It's a Battle Worth Fighting.

Some fights don't make headlines.

They happen behind closed doors. In doctor's offices. In quiet bedrooms. In the hearts of parents who rise every day to care for a child with special needs—and do it without applause, support, or rest.

I've seen it firsthand.

My nephew Zachary was born with Angelman Syndrome. He couldn't speak. Required full-time care. But he was radiant. Joyful. A light in every room. Yet as he grew, the care demands became crushing. My stepsister's world slowly closed in—friends disappeared, church became unmanageable, and she was left to carry it all alone.

That story should never happen.

But it happens every day.

One of my best friends from high school, Pastor Craig Johnson and his wife Sam, lived it too. His son Connor was diagnosed with autism. Craig was preaching to thousands at one of the largest churches in America… but his own family couldn't attend. There was no place for them. No support. Just silent suffering. Until Craig said, *"Enough."*

That's when **Champions Club** was born.

Champions Club is a global, faith-based program built to serve children, teens, and adults with special needs. Spiritually. Emotionally. Physically. Creatively. It gives families what they so often lack: hope, support, and a place where their child is not just accommodated—but celebrated.

When I saw the impact, I couldn't look away.

I joined the board. I offered to help turn Craig and Sam's story into a movie. And now, I've written this book to push the mission forward in a new way.

Because *The New Rules of Marketing Warfare* isn't just about business.

It's about **underdogs who refuse to give up**.

It's about **families who fight in silence—and deserve to be seen**.

It's about **building something bigger than a brand—it's building belonging**.

And now, you're part of the story.

Even if you're not a founder, entrepreneur, or marketer—**by buying this book, sharing it, or gifting it, you are funding Champions Foundation**. Every Amazon sale helps launch new Champions Clubs in communities that can't afford them.

But don't stop there.

Donate directly at championsclub.com

Scan the QR code below to give now.

Or go all in—**fund a Champions Club** at your church, school, or anywhere the need is great.

Because the world needs more than strategies.

It needs soldiers of hope.

It needs people willing to fight for the forgotten.

It needs Champions.

Join the mission. Be the movement. Fight for the ones who can't fight alone.

Scan to Give Hope!